The Ninth Level of Enlightenment

THE WISDOM OF THE LIGHT

BILL TORTORELLA

ISBN 979-8-88616-526-5 (paperback)
ISBN 979-8-88616-527-2 (digital)

Christian Faith Publishing
832 Park Avenue
Meadville, PA 16335
www.christianfaithpublishing.com

Printed in the United States of America

A special thanks to Madison Prieto for helping
with the editing of this book.

For life and death are one, Even as the river and sea are one. In the depth of your hopes and desires lies your silent knowledge of the beyond; And like the seeds dreaming beneath the snow, your heart dreams of spring. Trust the dreams, For in them is the hidden gate to eternity.

—Kahlil Gibran, *The Prophet*

For God so loved the world, he gave his only son,
that who ever believes in him should not perish but have eternal life.

—John 3:16

CHAPTER 1

Emergency Call Turned into a Miracle

I was asleep at F station, North Miami Beach, Florida. It was 2:00 a.m. on a warm night in the mean season; there are always big storms in Miami in the summer. The alarm rang, and I was awaken. I found out that we had less than two minutes to respond. Our last call was at 10:30 p.m., and we had just gotten back to the station at 12:15 a.m. I felt like I had just fallen into a deep sleep, and now, my colleague Jimmy and I were both back in our unit. Jimmy and I were paramedics.

I picked up the call on the mic, and the dispatcher said, "You have a 341 at 2755 E 137th Street, North Miami Beach."

F station was on 118th Street and 7th Avenue. The call was at 137th and 10th Avenues, making our response time less than ten minutes. I looked to my counterpart and said, "Jimmy, let's go."

And off we went. A call number that begins with a three is an emergency. Someone was badly ill, hurt, or sick, possibly a heart attack or stroke. Jimmy drove. Traffic was clear since it was so late at night, but the roads were dangerously wet and slick from the storm.

As we arrived at the house, I noticed that the door appeared to be open and mentioned this to him. Jimmy said, "I'm going to knock anyway."

Standard practice—since you never knew what you were walking into. For all we knew, it could have been someone with a gun. Jimmy knocked, and no one answered.

I opened the door slightly and called out, "Is anyone there?"

I heard a woman's voice in the back room. She announced, "We're back in the bedroom. Come inside!"

We opened the door to see a dark room, the bedside table filled with different medications. The woman was standing in the bathroom, and the husband, probably in his mid-sixties, was lying down on the bed. When I saw him, I knew he was probably having a stroke since he could not move one side of his body, and the right side of his face was caved in and drooping slightly. His pulse and blood pressure were very high, and he was clearly getting worse.

His wife informed us that he wanted to go to the VA hospital. "Ma'am, the VA hospital is over thirty-five minutes away," I said, "I can tell that your husband does not have that much time. I think it would be best to go directly to North Miami General Hospital. It's only about five minutes away."

She began yelling at us, insisting that we take him to the VA.

"Mrs. Larson, what is your husband's name?" I asked as I pulled her to the side.

"John," she answered.

I emphasized to her how serious his condition was and that he was deteriorating rapidly. I turned and spoke to John directly now: "John, we want to bring you right to North Miami General. It's five minutes from here."

At that time, John could still speak a bit out of one side of his mouth. He said, "Take me to the VA."

No way should we have attempted a half-hour-plus drive under the circumstances, but unfortunately, the rule at that time was different than it is today. You had to take the patient to whichever hospital they wanted to go to.

Like it or not, we began our journey to the VA hospital in downtown Miami. By the time we got John into the ambulance, he couldn't even talk. We hadn't even driven more than a couple of blocks when he went into respiratory arrest. I started an airway down his throat and started breathing for him with an Ambu bag and oxygen supply. He still had a pulse—weak but still there. By the time we reached I-95, he had entered full cardiac arrest, and his heart had stopped. It took us another twenty-five minutes to get to the VA hospital. I was doing full CPR on him all the way there. Keep in mind, his heart and breathing had fully stopped. I was keeping his heart pumping by hand and was breathing for him. At the same time, I was talking out loud, "Lord Jesus, help me."

We arrived at the VA, and the only staff on duty was the night nurse at her station up front. We rolled him in, and I yelled out, "Full cardiac arrest!"

The nurse jumped up and went back to get the attending doctor on duty. I asked Jimmy, "Didn't you call this in as a 341?" and he said that he had.

"I called it into the VA, but they didn't respond. I called three times—full cardiac arrest, code blue, no response. Maybe our radio was malfunctioning," he insisted.

I told him that I believed him, and I shouted to another nurse to call the respiratory therapist. She immediately called the respiratory therapists present in the hospital. Now they were on their way. I had a patient on the verge of death, and there was no time to waste.

The ER doctor eventually came running in, and I reiterated to him that we had called this in as a full cardiac arrest. I was sweating profusely by now, as I was still doing the CPR on John, continually yelling out to him, "Come on, John, come on!"

The doctor, after a few minutes, had prepared an epinephrine shot. He came over and administered the shot right into his heart. After sixty tense, crawling seconds later, John's heart started up right under my hands, like a locomotive. I was pushing down, and it was beating up. I called to the doctor and exclaimed, "He's got a pulse! He's got a pulse!"

The doctor pulled me away and put his stethoscope on his chest. He turned to us, smiled, and said, "Boys, he's back."

With man, this is impossible, but with God all things are possible.

—Matthew 19:26 (AVS)

The feeling that I had overwhelmed me—one of the most intense things that I had ever felt in my entire life. There is no adequate way to describe how you feel when you've just brought someone back that was dead for over thirty minutes. It's absolutely exhilarating.

Jimmy looked over to me and said, "Billy, you're soaking wet."

I looked down at myself and realized I was dripping, not from the rain but from sweat. Doing CPR for over thirty minutes is like a high-intensity workout. My adrenaline was still flying. I responded, "Jimmy, let's go to the break room and get something cold to drink."

A couple of nurses that we knew were there—Jean and Marcia. Jean asked what kind of call we brought in.

"We had a full cardiac arrest, and no one was in the emergency room. Jimmy called in a code blue three times and said there was no response," I explained. "Our radio wasn't working properly, no respiratory therapist, only one nurse was on duty, even the doctor was asleep in the break room."

Marcia said that she had no idea we were coming in. The fear that the call from our radio that Jimmy made may have not went through set in. I shrugged it off though—all was good, John was back. I started telling the girls the whole story. The wife demanding that we take him to the VA, doing CPR on John at seventy miles per hour down the I-95 highway, trying to hold my balance because the unit was slipping and sliding on the wet roads, how I had to put my leg under the side seat to try to stabilize myself.

What a call. I was still in shock on the way back to the station.

CHAPTER 2

I Fell into a Daydream

During the ride back, partly due to my physical exhaustion and partly due to the intensity of the scene I just had to witness, I started to daydream.

I asked myself, "How did I get here?"

Three years ago, I was graduating from the school of art and design in New York City with a commercial advertising degree. I was still attending the Art Student League in Manhattan and working for Triad Studios, a subset of Benton & Bowles, one of the biggest advertising firms in the city at that time.

Before I graduated, the school hosted a big contest for a storyboard concept; we had to create seventeen oil paintings on ten-by-thirty-inch panels, and they had to tell a complete story. I picked the story of Jesus Christ. What could be better than the greatest story ever told? I planned to paint the manger scene on the first panel and continue to depict events of his life until I reached the crucifixion, which I would paint on the last panel.

I did so much research. I read the Bible. I watched movies, like the *King of Kings*. I put my blood, sweat, and tears into these oil paintings for an entire semester. It was a ton of work, but time felt like it flew while I was painting. I was enjoying myself; painting is my passion.

I remember the day I dropped off all seventeen pieces. I set them all up on the display table, and my teacher at that time, Mr. Hollingsworth, inspected them and said, "Beautiful! What's your connection?"

"Love, Jesus is love," I responded.

"What inspiration. Excellent, excellent!" he said.

Mr. Hollingsworth himself had sponsored the contest. The winning set would earn the right to display their seventeen pieces on the street-facing windows of the school. About 200 students had entered their own work, and I ended up getting the first place. In the beginning of June, Mr. Hollingsworth displayed all seventeen of my panels to the streets of New York City. Back in those times, any exposure you could get as an artist was valuable; artists would pay thousands of dollars to have their work displayed in galleries, and here I was with seventeen original pieces of my artwork being shown to hundreds of thousands of passersby just because I did the work. It was a wonderful feeling, being on the other side of that, aside from the exposure though. People stopped and stared at my work, marveling at the life and story of Jesus. I was honored to have provided the vessels that might have gotten people thinking about God.

It was the summer of 1971 now. I had just graduated from the school of art and design. Unbelievable timing, as one day, soon after graduation, I was listening to our local radio station and heard that they were sponsoring a contest to promote Andrew Lloyd Webber's new rock opera musical, *Jesus Christ Superstar*. The contest was to design a card in celebration of the musical and the birthday of the radio station. There would be three winners that would be awarded: one for the largest card, one for the smallest card, and one for the most artistic card.

That night, my mind started to race. I couldn't wait to get started the next morning. I went straight to the lumberyard in the morning, and I came home dragging two four feet by eight feet plywood boards and a set of three hinges. My mother saw me as I came through the door in our apartment, and she shook her head, "Billy, what are you going to do now?"

I knew exactly what I was going to do. I was going to paint the picture that I could already see in my mind. I saw Jesus standing seven feet high with his arms spread out in love, with hundreds of people standing behind him—some holding crosses and torches, some cripples that were holding canes—as they fled their burning town on the top of the mountain. As they reached the bottom of the mountain, they reached out for Jesus and his love. And he gave it to them. Jesus was the healer, the teacher, the Son of God.

I had no way to know that there would be over 250,000 contestants in that contest, but I didn't care. I felt drawn to enter.

I spent weeks working on the card. I loved the fact that I had just worked on an exhibition of the life of Jesus and that I now had the opportunity to do it again.

When I brought my art to the NBC building in New York City, I brought my cousin, Tommy, to help me. We were coming into the building, carrying this massive four-by-eight-foot card; there was no way I could do it on my own. They had a ballroom in the NBC building where they had me set my card right in the middle of the room. One of the ladies who worked for NBC asked me to stand it up and open it. The card had the painting on the outside, and on the inside, it said:

Happy Birthday, Jesus Christ Superstar
WNBC

As we struggled, I saw someone that I recognized. After looking a bit harder, I realized who it was, and I couldn't believe my eyes. I saw Kirk Douglas, one of my favorite actors at that time, on his way out. All I could think was, *Spartacus! I'm standing in front of Spartacus!*

Mr. Douglas said, "That's a beautiful painting, son."

I said, "Thank you, Mr. Douglas. I did it for the new play *Jesus Christ Superstar*."

We exchanged a few more casualties, and then he was on his way. As he walked away, he left me feeling as if the sun was shining inside of my body. A movie star of his status, seeing my art and paying even a shred of attention to me? I couldn't believe it.

Two months later, I received a call from WNBC, hearing the words that I won for the most artistic card. I couldn't believe it— two months of waiting for the judges to go through 250,000 other entries, the anticipation mounting day by day, hoping and praying for another chance to show what I could do, and there I was, hearing that I had won!

I ended up scaring the pants off my mother. She thought I had fallen off a ladder or that the whole apartment building was about to come down with how I was jumping and yelling out of excitement. Once she realized what was happening though, she joined right in.

I was mostly excited about getting to be interviewed on television by NBC. It was an incredible opportunity since it was a wonderful form of advertising for your artwork. This was just like being able to showcase my work in the windows of the college of art and design but with so many more eyes. Remember that there was no social media, no internet, no way to get your art in front of people without it being there physically in front of them, and now, it was going to be put on television!

I wanted to let the television audience know how inspired I was about my story and how great it was to get do this project after I just finished the whole series of paintings about Jesus's life for school.

When the day finally came, it was so exciting! My girlfriend, Angela, and I arrived at WNBC about an hour before the interview. We headed into the ballroom, and I was astounded. There were so many cards. "Over 250,000!" was the response that I got when I asked the lady helping us how many there were. Her name was Janet. My card was standing right where I left it in the middle of the ballroom.

As the time moved forward, the excitement grew even more intensely. We were only ten minutes before the TV crew was due to arrive. I was a little nervous but, more so, thrilled. Just a little while later and all the people from the TV station and radio station were there waiting. It was going to be the best moment of my life—an opportunity to show my work live and to speak about it on national TV!

We waited and waited. It was now past the hour, and the film crew had not shown up. And everyone was getting a little antsy.

I saw Janet coming toward us at about twenty minutes past the hour with that dreaded look of disappointment on her face. She said, "Bill, the film crew was diverted to go to JFK airport. They had to cover Governor George Wallace coming into New York City."

I said, "Janet, what happened?"

"We're so sorry," she said. "Bill, don't be disappointed, you still won first prize out of 250,000 contestants, that's wonderful! And you have front-row orchestra tickets to one of the hottest shows of the year. You also have the backstage passes to meet the cast."

I can admit I was excited to meet Ben Vareen and some of the other actors.

"And besides that," she said, "remember your cash prize!"

I was very happy about this opportunity. All the prizes were fine and great, but I couldn't help but be disappointed about not being able to be interviewed. It was an incredible, once-in-a-lifetime chance to talk about my art, probably to the biggest audience I would ever be able to acquire. It was so important for me to be able to get my work out there and to talk about the story behind it. I honestly felt like I had been punched in the gut, but maybe, this was part of God's plan for me.

The night of the play came a few days later. It really was incredible, inspired by the greatest story ever told. The dancing and the singing were outstanding. What a play! This was, by far, the best show I'd ever seen. Being able to meet the actors and talk with them afterward was a gift on its own. It was just a wonderful and incredible night despite my disappointment a few days prior.

CHAPTER 3

The Move to Miami

Two years later, Angela and I were married at her church. Our reception was in a catering hall in Brooklyn. Between my family and her family, all our friends, and all my father's friends from the union, it was packed and a lot of fun. I sang "The Impossible Dream" with the band for my mother. It brought on a lot of tears of happiness.

We left for the Bahamas the next morning. It was a beautiful honeymoon. We got to spend our first week of marriage on Paradise Island. We went scuba diving, had some great dinners, did a little bit gambling in the casino. I was pretty lucky there. Actually, I won $1,500!

After the honeymoon, we went home to Brooklyn, but we had already decided that we were moving to Florida. It was a long, brutal process, but we were newly married and were ready to begin our lives together somewhere new. We got ready, borrowed my mother's big Cadillac, stuffed it to the brim with all our belongings, and began the long drive down to the Sunshine State.

When Angela and I arrived in Florida, it was like a paradise to us. We looked at so many different locations to live. We tried Fort Lauderdale first, unknowingly arriving in the middle of spring break. On the beach, there were college students partying there, getting wasted, hanging from balconies, driving drunk, and engaging in a slew of other reckless actions. We knew we couldn't live there.

We finally picked out a beautiful area in North Miami Beach; it was close to the beach and not far from Downtown Miami, where I could easily find a job in advertising commercial artwork, and Angela would be able to find a job as a legal secretary. We found a perfect little one-bedroom garden apartment. We had a pool right outside our door that was surrounded by palm trees. I felt like I was in heaven.

I had run into a little luck in the Bahamas and won $1,500 in the casino, and we had about $7,500 in wedding gifts. Keep in mind that $7,500 back then was equivalent to about $50,000 today. We had more then we needed to get started. We bought a nice blue convertible Mustang for $2,500. We bought furniture for the living room, bedroom, and dining room and a TV. In total, we had spent about $4,000 in our first few weeks, and we had $3,500 left. We thought we would take one more week before we went to look for jobs.

In my youthful naivete, I had the brilliant idea that Angela and I should go back to the Bahamas for the weekend. I foolishly thought I could make us a little more money in the casino. Angela didn't think it was a good idea and hesitated. But I eventually convinced her to say yes when I told her that I would only take $1,000 with me and leave the rest at home. We immediately called Chalk's International Airlines and booked a flight for the weekend.

We took a seaplane with only eight other people on board and landed right in the water between Nassau and Paradise Island. The plane pulled right onto the shore of Paradise Island. We cleared customs in ten minutes, and we were in the hotel lobby, checking in, five minutes later. By this point, it was late in the afternoon. Angela and I had dinner at our favorite Bahamian steak house, ate exquisite steaks, salads, escargot, and flambé for dessert. We were really living large.

Friday night was great. Angela went to play some slots. I went ahead and sat down at the blackjack table and was up and down for a couple of hours. I was playing the dice tables after some time had passed, and Angela came up to me and told me that she had won $100 on the slot machines. In our excitement, we decided to go to the dance club next door. It was Friday-night fever time. We spent the rest of the night dancing, having fun. I was down a little bit, so we broke out close to even for the night. I couldn't wait to make some more money the next night.

The next day, we went out scuba diving. We went to the beach to get some sun. We took a nap. We were having an incredible time. By the time the evening rolled around, after dinner, we were ready to head back to hit the jackpot and went straight back to the casino.

I never told Angela I had the rest of our wedding gifts, $3,500, on me. I thought that since last time I was here I won $1,500, I could make it big with some more money to start out. I knew that she wouldn't approve, so I didn't tell her.

Angie went off to play her slots, and I went to play the dice tables. I remembered the people that I was playing with at the same table three weeks ago. They were making bigger bets, taking in lots of money. One man off my roll of the dice must have taken in at least $30,000. It all had to do with your betting skills. So I cashed $1,500 in chips. I got ten black $100 chips and twenty green $25 chips.

Well—that was all gone in less than an hour. So instead of walking away, I took another $1,500 out of my pocket.

Two hours later, that was gone.

Now I was down by $3,000, thinking I had $500 left, forgetting the fact that I was down $200 from the night before. That's when I could hear my father's voice say, "Don't be young and dumb."

If only I had heard that voice after the first $1,500.

I went to get Angela and said, "Let's get out of here." I was praying that she won some money. "How did you do Angie?" I asked.

"I lost $200," she said discouraged.

"How much do you have left?"

"About $30."

The next day, we left. After tipping the bellman and the taxi, we had $300. As if my conscience wasn't tormenting enough, I had forgotten that the Bahamas had a $25 exit tax for each person traveling.

Now we were down to about $250.

With no jobs, we arrived back home in Miami with Angela thinking we still had $2,500 in the house and me kicking myself because I knew that we really had no money left. The next morning at breakfast, I told her.

"I lost it all," I said.

She said, "I know, I can't believe we lost $1,000!"

I said, "No, I lost it all."

Angie lost it. She was so angry, and understandably so. She thought we would have to call our parents and have them send down some money.

I said, "We'll try to get by with the $250 that we have left."

She told me that she was ashamed of me. I felt that way too.

The same day, the electric company called and said that I would have to come down to the office with $90 for the transfer fee, or else, they would turn our power off. I had no idea about that. I thought the electricity was included in the apartment! At that point, I realized that we only had $160 to live on, and neither of us had jobs.

A light bulb clicked on in my head. I had made us become the friends that I had back in Brooklyn, with no food in the refrigerator and no way to get more. I had made us become what I spent my whole life trying not to be. In my mind, I was already thinking of ways that I could make money *fast*.

It was then that I began to toy with the idea of biting the bullet, telling my father about everything and having him just send down some money. After a bit of thought, I told Angie that we were just going to have to figure it out. My dad was the president of one of the biggest Teamster's Union locals in New York City. If I told him I lost all the money at the casino, he would have sent my uncle Paul down, and I'd have to go into hiding. Even though my uncle Paul loved me, he would have broken both my legs—that was just how things were taken care of back in the day. Sure they would have bailed me out in the end, but I didn't want to play with that idea at all.

A few days later, Angela had found a good job as a secretary for a big company out in Hialeah, Florida. It was only about a twenty-minute drive to work. She would be getting great pay, and it would be fulfilling for her, but she wasn't getting paid her first paycheck until two weeks later. That was a big problem.

In 1973, Miami was not the big city that I expected it to be. There I was, a young man, thinking that every big city had advertising firms, but I was wrong—there were none. Miami hadn't been converted to the hottest vacation spot on the planet yet. I had a very good portfolio working on *CoverGirl* ads in New York City. My first thought was to head straight to the *Miami Herald*—they *had* to have an art department! I called and made an appointment for Wednesday, two days later, at 10:00 a.m.

When the day came, I was ready to knock 'em dead. I had my suit and tie on, and I arrived thirty minutes early. After a couple of very nervous minutes in the waiting room, an older man opened his office door, and the secretary nudged me in. The man had a nice big office with lots of awards that covered the walls. "Let's see your portfolio, son," he said.

I placed it on his desk, and he began to finger through it. He would periodically look up at me then back down at my portfolio. It was a very quiet, tense few minutes. Once, he looked up at me and said, "Very good work, young man."

I hadn't even said anything, and he was impressed. I let my work speak for me. I was ecstatic. All the nerves were gone—how could he pass me up for this job?

"I'm very sorry," he said, and my heart dropped. "We just, yesterday, filled the position you wanted. That was the only job available."

I sat there in disbelief; would I ever get some good news?

The interviewer actually advised me to go back home to New York or to Chicago because that's where the big advertising agencies were and that I would have more luck up there. I felt devastated as I left the building. There was no way I was going to go back to New York! I was in Miami now, and I was there to stay.

I became so desperate that I started knocking on doors at print houses to see if they had any freelance work as they were printing brochures for new houses and condominiums—but no luck. I went home to my wife that night and told her that it wasn't looking good for me.

I think this was the first time in my life I had truly felt depression. Angela looked at me and said that we were down to our last $30 and we had no food in the apartment. It couldn't get any worse than this. Good thing I at least filled the car with gas. But we had to eat, so I went to the supermarket and bought a 50¢ bag of potatoes and some condiments: butter, ketchup, salt, and pepper. We had about eight days until Angela would get paid. She thought about asking her boss for an advance. I told her that I didn't think that would look good. First of all, she didn't know him well enough.

"We can make it," I said, "I'll think of something."

Angela disagreed. We had new bills coming, and even after she got paid, we wouldn't have had enough to pay them. I wasn't going to let my new wife live in poverty and worry about being able to pay the bills. I told her, "Look at me. I will find a way to get the bills paid."

I told myself that I would have to do something fast to get us through. That night, I prayed to God to help us get through this.

"If you can?" Said Jesus. "Everything is possible for one who believe."

—Mark 9:23 (NIV)

CHAPTER 4

Miracles at the Dog Track

After spending all night thinking about what to do, I went to Yellow Taxicab Company in Miami that next day, Thursday. They told me that they didn't need any new drivers. Now I pleaded with the manager, "Please! Something must be available? I need work."

He looked at me sympathetically, then started writing something down on a piece of paper and handed it to me. He said to me, "Go see John at White Taxicab Company in North Miami Beach on Biscayne Boulevard and 128th Street."

I went over immediately, and I introduced myself to John. He looked to me to be in his fifties, wearing a white shirt that was too small for his belly; the buttons were being pulled apart. He looked at me with a cigar hanging out the side of his mouth, and he said, "You pay me the first $50 that you make every day, and then you get 50 percent of the meter for whatever you take in for the rest of the day." He also told me, "If you only take in $40 one day, then the next day, you owe me $60."

"When can I start?" I asked.

"My name is Bill Tortorella. I need to feed my wife and I."

Flash forward to 5:00 p.m., and I was picking up Angela from work. I had her drive me back to the taxi company and told her that I would be back whenever I was done working. Just like that, she dropped me off and went home for the night. Now when I got back to the White Taxi Cab Company, John asked me how well I knew Miami.

"Well, just from driving around, looking for jobs," I responded, "I know the highways and the major boulevards, and I'm pretty good with the streets and avenues. I can always look directions up on a map."

He had a pleased look on his face. He went into his drawer, looked around a bit, and pulled a beautiful map of Miami and its surrounding towns. The map was easy to read, and I could see everything. He handed the map to me and told me that they had a designated lineup at the Miami International Airport, Miami dog track, and the Gulfstream racetrack with their company's taxi stands. He said that the other drivers would show me where they were.

It was 6:00 p.m. by then, and John said, "You're losing time. Drive down to the airport, you will be eighth out. That will give you time to get down there."

I took on twelve-hour shifts so I could make some more money. The week had already gone by, and Angela was about to be paid. Now it's nighttime. I took my first fare at the airport. It was to Ninth Street and Collins Avenue Miami Beach. After that, I figured out the best spots where I could pick up good rides.

I came in early that Friday afternoon, I picked up my taxi, and I drove right over to the Miami airport. I was in line for about forty minutes until I finally got called in to pick up a ride. I pulled up to the terminal, and I saw a lot of luggage out there, so I jumped out of the car, ran around to pick it up, and put it in the trunk.

"Hi, Billy."

I looked up, and it was an old girl friend of mine from high school. We never officially dated, the timing was never right, and she always seemed to have a boyfriend, but I liked her a lot at that time.

"Hi, Denise," I said gingerly.

"How are you?" she asked.

17

"I'm just doing fine, just driving that cab down here for a while and doing some of my oil paintings for some art galleries."

Denise was a rich, beautiful girl. I was so embarrassed. Here I was, driving a taxicab, when I graduated at the top of my class. I was ready to conquer the world then.

She got in the taxi, and she was very nice to me. I took her to her father's home in Miami Beach. I told her that I was working for Benton & Bowles in New York City, how, after I got married, we moved down to Miami on a whim, a spur of the moment idea, and how, when we arrived down here, I found out they had no advertising agencies, so it was very hard for me to find something to do for work. When I dropped her off, I felt like crap. I felt like I had failed.

We arrived at her father's home, and I stepped out of the car to start unloading her luggage. She could probably tell how embarrassed I was and how down I was feeling, so she gave me a big hug before we said goodbye. I drove away with tears rolling down my face.

I was very upset, but I drove over to Miami dog track and waited on the taxi line. It looked like it was coming down to the last race. I haven't picked up a fare yet. I was feeling pretty bad about myself. I didn't know it, but I was visually upset. I got called in to pick up my fare, and a couple got in the car. The man and woman were both dressed to the nines. The man had a great-looking white suit and a cool hat on, and his lady was dressed beautifully.

He took one look at me and said, "What's the matter? It looks like you're having bad day." He had an English accent that instantly woke me from my slumber.

I said, "No, I just had a wake-up call today." I told the story about meeting Denise and how it made me feel sorry about myself. I told them everything. I couldn't stop myself. I told them about how seeing her made me feel pretty bad about myself, that I had different plans, and here I was, driving a taxicab in Miami. I told them about how I had lost all the money my wife and I received from our wedding gifts in the Bahamas.

"What island were you on?" he asked.

I told him that we were on Paradise Island and that I had lost all the money in the Paradise Island casino. I kept on rambling. I said that I was too embarrassed to call home for money. I don't know if it was their accents, but they seemed to actually feel bad for me. I said to them, "Are you from England?"

He said, "We are from the Bahamas."

Right then, I was pulling up to their hotel downtown Miami. I said I was sorry for unloading all my problems on them. After I realized that, that was exactly what I had done. I felt terrible. The well-dressed man looked at me and said, "Billy, everything is going to be all right for you." Then he turned and said something to his wife. He then said, "Billy," like he knew me.

"We didn't introduce ourselves, but my name is Nigel Nottage, and this is Miss Rosemary." Nigel said, "Billy, if you don't mind waiting for us a bit while we get ready for dinner about an hour. We want to go out to a nice restaurant. Keep the meter running."

I said, "Of course! I'll wait right over here."

It was a little after 6:00 p.m. when they came down. They looked great, so sharply dressed. Nigel had on a powder-blue suit, and Miss Rosemary had on a white dress that flowed in the wind. As they got in the car, Nigel said, "I want you to take us to a steak house I know. It's on Biscayne Boulevard."

And off we went. He was giving me the directions, as I had never been there. They began talking about themselves, and I was fascinated by them living in Nassau. I asked Nigel what he did for a living.

"I'm a personal lawyer for Mr. Howard Hughes," he said.

I, in shock, said, "The flying Dutchman Howard Hughes?"

He said, "Yes, the one and only."

Now I was so interested in his story, but we had just pulled up to the restaurant.

I stopped the car, and Nigel told me to park the taxi in one of the restaurant parking spots. At this point, I had been driving for them for about two hours or more. John called over the radio and asked out loud if I was still with that run from the dog track. I responded with yes and that I didn't call in earlier because they were getting ready. Now John got on the radio, "Make sure you get some money out of these people!"

I was totally humiliated. Nigel calmly reached his head over the back seat and loudly asked me how much was on the meter so that John could hear, to which I was able to respond, "$140."

There was an awkward pause, and John came back on the radio and apologized.

Nigel then put four $100 bills in my hand and said, "Billy, you must be hungry."

I said, "Yes, but I'm not dressed. This place looks like a nice restaurant."

Nigel said, "Don't worry about that."

So I closed the taxi, and we went into the restaurant—the three of us. While waiting for the table, it became apparent that Nigel knew the maître d', as he walked up to him and asked, "Do you have a jacket for this young man?"

The maître d' said that he might have something. He disappeared into a back room, and he actually came out with a nice jacket. I put it on, and it fit like a glove.

I couldn't believe this. Here I was in a nice jacket in the company of the flying Dutchman's personal lawyer. Last week, I was only eating potatoes; now, I was in a fine steak house on Biscayne Boulevard about to eat steak and lobster and Caesar salad.

We were called to our table and sat down. Nigel asked me about where I attended school. I told Nigel about how I had graduated from the school of art and design in New York City and how I had studied advertising and illustration. I also told Nigel about the *Jesus Christ Superstar* card contest that had 250,000 other contestants that entered and that I was awarded first place for the most artistic card. I also went on to tell him about working for Benton & Bowles advertising agency in the city. I realized I was running my mouth and said, "Enough talking about me! I'm interested in finding out more about you and your business. Like the things you do for Mr. Howard Hughes."

Nigel replied, "Yes, I have worked strictly for Howard Hughes in the Bahamas for some time now." He said that Howard lived up in the top penthouse in the Britannia Towers Hotel on Paradise Island. From 1970 to 1972, he owned the top two floors with all its suites for all his staff, how he had occupied those floors for almost two years. He then told me about one night when Howard just picked up and left. He went to London for about a year.

I asked why he left, and Nigel said, "That's something I am not allowed to talk about. It falls under his attorney-client privilege."

About a year after he left the Bahamas, he returned. When he came back, he went to the Xanadu Princess Resort & Marina in Freeport, Bahamas. Nigel said that there were twelve suites on the twelfth floor and four suites on the top floor. Howard stayed on the top floor in one of the massive suites.

I found out years later that, at that time, Hughes was being investigated by the IRS because he had evidently donated $100,000 to the Richard Nixon reelection campaign, and this all took place when Nixon was being investigated by the United States Senate about the Watergate incident. I read in an article something about the $100,000 that was to buy Howard Hughes favors in the Bahamas. He owned hundreds of prime acres of beachfront property. Everyone thought he was going to build on it.

Nigel also said something very curious to me over dinner, and I didn't quite understand it. He had said, "Billy, you're going to be a merchant and buy and sell goods all over the world. Your business will take you on many travels, and you will be very successful."

I jokingly said, "When do I start?"

The meal was excellent; the company was even better. We all got back in the taxi, and I said, "Where to, Nigel?"

He responded, "We're going back to the dog track for the evening races."

It was quiet for a while until we got to the dog track. I guess we were all in a food coma from all that great food.

We arrived at the dog track, and I thought I was just going to be drop them off and say goodbye. As we arrived, Nigel said, "Drive over to valet."

I said, "Nigel, why would I drive over the valet?"

He said, "Well, we want to valet park the car."

"The taxi—you want me to valet park the taxi?" I asked, dumbfounded.

"Absolutely," he responded, "We're going to the clubhouse."

I pulled up to the valet, got out, and handed the valet my keys. The valet guy looked at me funny.

I shrugged my shoulders and said, "He's the boss," as I gestured toward Nigel.

We went on up to the clubhouse. They were having some drinks. I helped myself to a beer, as we were enjoying watching the dog races. Five races went by, and before the sixth race, Nigel looked at me and asked, "Billy, what are your lucky numbers? Give me three."

I said the numbers that first came to my mind—three, one, and five. Three-one-five was my old address number back in Brooklyn. Nigel left to go to the ticket window and came back with six $12 box tickets on three, one, and five. He threw down the tickets on the table, and then we heard the announcer say, "Here's Bunny!"

And the dogs were off. Dog numbers three and one were in good position, but I didn't hear anything from the announcer about dog number five until the final turn, when they announced. He started yelling, "It's yellow dog eats number five, and it's yellow dog eats! Yellow dog eats in the final eighth! Yellow dog eats takes the lead!"

The race finished—five, three, then one. Nigel had six trifecta tickets now that paid $710 each—that was $4,260 Nigel just won. I was so happy for him. I said, "Nigel, you won!"

He said, "Billy, what do you mean? We won!"

Nigel turned around and counted out $2,130 and handed it to me. Today, that would be like someone handed you $20,000 dollars.

I thought, *God sent this angel to me.* I was shaking and tears were rolling down my eyes. It felt like everything was moving in slow motion. Rosemary was jumping up and down, and she said to me, "Billy, tomorrow night, take your wife out for a beautiful dinner."

We stayed for one more race, and then we left. Nigel turned around and told me, "You always walk away a winner."

We all left the dog track very happy that night. We came out with pockets full of money. When we reached the hotel, the meter read $462. Nigel asked me what it was at, but I said, "$462, but Nigel, forget it, you have already given me more than I could ever expect." I had the $400 from earlier and the $2,100. I had $2,500 to bring home to Angela!

Nigel and his wife got out of the taxi, and I just took a minute to take the meter off. Nigel knocked on the passenger window. I put it down, and he said, "Billy, you remember what we talked about over dinner in the restaurant, right?"

I said, "Yes, we talked about me being in my own business someday as a merchant."

And then he dropped another $700 on the seat and walked away.

I yelled out to him, "Nigel! This is too much!"

He said, "Billy, that's a good start for you. You lost $3,200 in the casino. Enjoy your life."

I went home that night, and I tossed $3,200 across our bed. Angela shot up in utter disbelief, and I said, "God blessed us. This was something miraculous." I didn't remember telling him how much I lost. I told him I lost the money, yes, but I never did say how much. I remember my mom saying to me that everything happens for a reason. At that moment, I knew an angel was watching over me. This was 1973—$3,200 was a lot of money. And that was the exact amount I lost in the Bahamas. It came back to me from the Bahamas.

Whatever you ask for in prayer believe you
have received it, and it will be yours.
And when you stand praying, if you hold
anything against anyone, forgive them,
so that your father in Heaven may forgive you for your sins.

—Jesus Christ, Mark 11:24–25 (NIV)

CHAPTER 5

Red Reef Park and the Power of Prayer

I snapped out of my daydream as we arrived back to the station. A lot had happened in the last few years for me, and it was good to think back and reflect on it from time to time. We went inside, and Jimmy went to lie down and rest, but I was still so excited about bringing John back, and it was almost time to change shifts, so I went outside to clean the unit up and get it ready for the new crew coming on at 7:00 a.m.

I couldn't wait to get home that morning; it was Saturday, and Angela and I had a plan to go to the beach for the day. We used to go to Red Reef Park up in Boca Raton to snorkel. The reef was right off the beach, and it was beautiful. Angela drove, and I told her the whole story about the call the night before with John. She asked why John's wife wouldn't let us take him to North Miami General Hospital.

"Honey, I don't know." I didn't want to think or talk about it anymore. Right then, the reef was on my mind, and I needed a day of relaxation.

It was a beautiful sunny day, and the water was crystal clear and calm, heavily shaded with palm trees. We claimed one of the picnic tables and filled the barbecue stand with charcoal since we had friends coming down to meet us at noon: one of the other paramedic drivers that I work with, Nick Dunn, and his wife, Sue. And then we were off to do some snorkeling.

The water was perfect that day. It was warm. The visibility was very good, and there were fish all around—parrotfish, angelfish, barracuda, a couple of lobsters. After about thirty minutes, Angela was tired and headed back on the beach to get some sun. I just kept on snorkeling; it was my serenity. A nice, calm day in the water makes the world feel like a beautiful place again. It would take my mind off all the accidents, the heart attacks, and the shootings. I loved it. As I was heading back to the beach, a giant nurse shark swam right up near me. It was only a couple of feet away. By the time I got out, I was like a prune. I must have been in the water for over three hours.

But it was lunchtime, and the barbecue was working. I could hear my friend Nick's voice from the beach. He already had the hamburgers and hot dogs on the grill. He ended up surprising us as he'd bought some nice steaks. I started telling stories and some funny jokes and listened to some good music. The day went by too quickly.

Angela and I arrived home that night around 7:00 p.m., and I was out cold for the rest of the night. Before I knew it, it was 5:00 a.m. Sunday morning, and I was getting ready to go back at work. This was a tough week. We were working a lot of double shifts. I took a shower, made some breakfast, and then I was off to the station.

We picked up all our units at the main station in Downtown Miami, then we would all drive to our own stations. I always got there a little early to have my coffee and do a double-check on the units to make sure they were stocked up and ready to go. I did my checklist, hopped in front of the unit with Jimmy, and we were off to F station in North Miami Beach.

This particular morning, something supernatural stepped in. We got on I-95, heading North to 125th Street, where F station was, when we heard a call. We were on Seventy-ninth Street and I-95; the call came over the radio. It was for a car accident—two possible injuries. I picked up the speaker and said, "This is unit 67 D. Our location is Seventy-ninth Street, exit on I-95, heading North. Can you please repeat back the accident?"

The dispatcher said that there was a 317 on 135th Street northbound I-95.

I said, "Pull that call from 69 D. We have a two-minute ETA."

So the dispatcher called up 69 D, my buddy Pete Paine's unit, and told them to stand down.

"Sixty-seven D is on the call. They have a two-minute ETA."

By the time I stop talking, we were already at 120th Street. It actually took us only two minutes to get there. When we arrived at the scene, it was apparent that the accident was very bad. It looked like a white Chevy Nova had run full speed into the back of a big pickup truck. There was a man in the truck and a younger man running around in panic.

I hopped out of our unit with medical equipment, and the young man at the scene was crying, "My sister! My sister! Help her!"

Hurrying over to the car, I saw his sister's head had gone through the front windshield. Half of her head was on the inside, the other half on the outside, and it looked like the windshield itself was lodged into her skull. I feared that she might already be dead because there was so much blood. Just then, I saw some movement from her arm.

I had to make a quick assessment. There was so much blood loss that we decided to take her off instead of waiting for the fire truck to cut her out. If we waited, she would die. Jimmy and I proceeded to take her very carefully off the windshield. We got her on the stretcher and put her directly into the unit. Her brother hopped in the back with me, bawling his eyes out, understandably so. Jimmy got into the driver's seat and took off.

I began looking to see if there was more glass stuck in her head. Luckily, we were only five minutes away from Pine's General Hospital. Thank God we didn't wait because the fire truck never arrived at the scene. I started to wonder about the man in the truck, why he never exited his car, but I shrugged it off pretty quick. I had work to do. Now I was applying some bandages to her head and trying to keep myself secure while Jimmy was driving. The siren was on, and we were rolling fast. I could see a little breathing still, but the blood was everywhere. Whenever there's a head injury of any kind, it bleeds profusely. Then she went into a seizure. She was thrashing so intensely, her body was jumping off the stretcher, and she was totally unconscious at the same time.

"God help me!" I called out. I told her brother to stand up and hold her legs down. I knew I couldn't control her by myself. I was holding down the top of her head, and all her bandages started coming off, and she began bleeding again. After what felt like the longest five minutes of my life, we arrived at Pine's General. All the nurses were out and ready to help. They ran her right into surgery. I kept on thinking, *God help her*. Pine's General was fortunately one of the better emergency hospitals to go to when you were close enough.

Jimmy and I both had a lot of blood all over us, so we went back to the station to take a shower and clean up and put on a new uniform. Our job was done there. When you get a call like that, it's horrific and hard not to think about it. I was reflecting on it all day. I tried to stop thinking about it.

Very rarely do you ever want to go back to ask the hospital what happened because when it's that bad, most of the time, the outcome is bad as well. But the next morning, I told Jimmy, "I feel like I have to go back to Pine's before we take the unit in."

It was out of our way, but I felt like I had to find out what happened to her. I told Jimmy that I needed to do this. I insisted. So Jimmy agreed but reluctantly. "Billy, I think she has passed away," he warned me.

I didn't care. I said, "Jimmy, let's go."

We arrived at Pine's General Hospital, and we walked up to one of the nurses that we knew. I said, "Dawn, what happened to the young girl that we brought in yesterday morning?"

"Why don't you go up to her room and introduce yourself?" she asked hintingly.

The chills ran through my body. I asked in disbelief, "She's still alive?"

Dawn responded and said, "I'll take you up to her room."

I was both in shock and filled with happiness for her. When we got in her room, she was sitting up in bed, her whole head bandaged up. Her brother ran over to me and gave me a big hug. He turned around to his sister and said to her, "This is the man that saved your life!"

She was so happy and, may I add, so lucky. I thanked God that he was listening to me when I called out to him in the ambulance. The young girl, Carol, did not have any kind of brain damage, nor did she have a skull fracture. All the blood was from her being scalped. So that was why we couldn't see anything—the skin on the top of her head was peeled back. I left the hospital feeling wonderful about the gift that God gave me to give back.

The purpose of Service is so God could reach others through our hands.

—Corinthians 9:12–13 (NIV)

CHAPTER 6

A Little Laughter Is a Blessing

Some days at the station, there was a lot of laughter. Our crew included Jimmy and I, Pete, Nick, John, and Manny. Pete was a comedian. Jimmy, my partner, was completely the straight guy. They were like a comedy team. Pete was always pulling pranks. My personal favorite was the day when Pete threw a red T-shirt in with Jimmy's white uniform. Jimmy took his uniform out of the washing machine, looked at it, and started yelling, "Pete Paine! You son of a bitch!" and started chasing him out the door, all the way down the block.

Pete was running down the street so fast. Jimmy was so mad. I think he would have thrown Pete in the lake. We were all standing outside, watching and laughing. Jimmy was the only medic that drove around with a pink uniform on for the rest of the month.

In the station, we had our own gym setup. We had a great card table and played a lot of poker in our downtime. In the kitchen, we all took turns cooking. I cooked the best Italian food because I came from a family that owned a restaurant and bar. Then we had Jimmy; he cooked Chilean food. Pete Paine cooked great barbecue, and Manny cooked awesome Cuban food.

At times, it was slow, and we would have big feasts. Sometimes, we would talk about the calls of the day. Not all of them were bad; some of them were actually pretty funny. You needed to have laughter with a job like ours; it healed the soul because, sometimes, what we saw on a daily basis was horrific. It's the kind of job where every day, you don't know what you're walking into. Heart attacks, strokes, car accidents, fire, and blood. So you definitely need some laughter in your life.

Jimmy and I had a call one afternoon at a four-story walk-up apartment building. We had a hard enough time carrying the stretcher up four flights. It was called in as a routine call to transfer a lady down to Kingston Memorial Hospital. We arrived at the apartment, and the door was open. I called in and said, "Is anybody home?"

I heard the lady say, "Yes, I'm in the back here!"

We went back to the bedroom and opened the door.

To my amazement, she was the size of her full-size bed. She must have been 600 pounds. Jimmy asked her what was wrong, and she said, "My bowels, my bowels! They're all clogged up. You have to take me to Kingston."

Now I was trying to figure out if we could even get her on the stretcher or if she would even fit through the doorway. She asked, "Are there only two of you today?"

I said, "Why? Do you call in often?"

"Yes, but they usually send four men," she replied.

I asked Jimmy if he thought we should call another unit because I thought Pete might be in the area. Jimmy said, "No, I think we should try by ourselves."

I headed back down to the unit and took out the extra belts we had from under the stretcher. I knew we were going to need some long extensions. Thank God we had plenty of them. When I walked back up, I said to the lady, "Ma'am, can you walk at all?"

She said, "No, but I could sit up."

She tried to sit, but as soon as she started to move, she started yowling in pain, "My bowels! My bowels!"

So we figured the best way would be to try to roll her on the stretcher. It was tough work with a lot of pained yelling, but we got her there. Now she was on the stretcher, hanging off all sides. Luckily, she wasn't that tall but, boy, was she big. I got all the belts out, handed some to Jimmy, and I took the belt and the extensions, trying to fit at least enough on so that we could get her legs and the top half of her body down securely. We got her strapped in so that she was lying on her side and began walking.

We got to the door, and we couldn't get her through.

I said, "Ma'am, how do they normally get you outside?"

She said, "They stuff me."

"What do you mean?" I asked.

"They push me out with their hands."

Jimmy and I then reluctantly started stuffing her as best as we could through her bedroom door. There was a lot of awkward squeezing and pushing, but eventually, we were able to get her through.

Now we had the apartment door. It seemed to be a little wider, so it was somewhat easier, but now, we were at the top of the staircase. I told Jimmy, "I'm a little bigger than you"—at that time, I thought I was strong enough to hold her back—"I'll take the top with the big handles. You get on the bottom and just try to hold her. Try to take her down one step at a time."

Well, we started rolling her, and soon as the back wheels on the stretcher cleared the top step and all the weight was hanging on my handles, the handles just popped right off. I yelled to Jimmy to get out of the way. She went *boom boom boom, bump bump bump* all the way down the staircase, and she stopped when she hit the wall.

I yelled out, "Ma'am! Are you all right?"

She yelled back, "Yes, I'm fine but my bowels! Get me to Kingston!"

We had to call in for a backup unit with two other men. They were able to help us get her down the rest of the stairs, up into our unit, and strap her in. We dropped her off on four gurney tables side by side at the hospital.

Most of these kinds of calls were handled by the private ambulance companies, but at times, we would have to take the routine overflow calls that came in.

One particular call, our buddy Pete Paine had a brand-new medic attendant, named Flarity, straight out of school. They had a routine call to pick up someone that had passed away in their apartment. Pete received the call and knew they would need masks or Vicks to put under their noses because when someone is dead and lying there for four days, the smell becomes awful. It might just be the worst smell you could possibly think of.

Pete, before they went in, put some Vicks under his nose but didn't tell Flarity to wear a mask or use the Vicks. Whether it was Pete being a prankster as usual or him just totally forgetting, I'll never know. When Pete and Flarity arrived in the apartment, the smell was intense, and Flarity felt ill almost instantly. After practically begging Pete a few times, Pete said he could go down to the unit and wait for them there. After Flarity left, Pete took his mask out of his pocket and put it on. The police officers in the room had gas masks on.

Now when someone dies in a sitting up position and is there for over four days, the rigor mortis had set in already three days before, so the body is stiff as a board in an L-shaped position. Pete asked the two police officers to help him to get the body onto the stretcher. They rolled it close to the side of the bed. They open the body bag up and were able to set him up on the stretcher and zip up the body bag. They helped him straighten out the body so he could apply the three belts required for that kind of transport.

Remember, the body is incredibly stiff, so when you pry the top half of the body down, it's like a spring and will bounce right back if nothing is holding it. The men pried down the body and tightened one belt right across the top of his chest, one on his lower stomach and one on the bottom of his legs. The police officers helped Pete out of the apartment and down to the unit.

By that time, Flarity felt a little better. He was there to help put him inside the unit. He nervously asked Pete if he could sit in the front seat on the way to the morgue, and Pete said, "No, you have to stay in the back and make sure the body is secure."

Even though the body was in the bag, there was still a hint of smell. Pete, having a little too much fun, took the extra time to drive down to the morgue. By the time they arrived and Pete opened the back doors to the unit, Flarity was gasping for air.

"Flarity, get out here," Pete said to him.

Flarity jumped out of the back, took some deep breaths, and Pete asked him if he was all right.

He said, "Yes, Pete, I'm fine," and was able to help Pete roll the body into the morgue.

When they got inside, Pete said to Flarity, "You don't have to help me pick him up," because Pete knew the top belt on his chest, once released, the body was going to spring right up. Pete said to Flarity, "Just do me a favor. If you don't mind, go over and unbuckle the belts. Start with the top one."

He walked to the top of the stretcher, bent over, and unlocked the belt. The body jumped up and hit Flarity in the head. Flarity then ran out the door, never to be seen again. He never even came back for his check. Pete couldn't catch him. He did feel bad for that one prank. He never expected Flarity to take off like that, but that was the nature of a Pete Paine prank.

A cheerful heart is good medicine. But a
crushed spirit dries up the bones.

—Proverbs 17:22 (ESV)

CHAPTER 7

Lady Down—341 Emergency Call

It was a late-afternoon call. Jimmy and I jumped in our unit. I picked up the mic, and the dispatcher told us that the address was 546 NW 196 Street, North Miami. I will never forget this day. It was a 341-emergency call, we were briefed to the best of the dispatcher's ability, but we could never be prepared to witness what we saw.

We arrived at the building, stepped in the apartment, and there was a lady in the bathroom. There was blood everywhere. She was lying on the floor, and I could see she was pregnant and lying down in a puddle of blood in a lot of pain.

I said, "Ma'am, how long have you been pregnant?"

She told me six months. I looked in the corner of the bathroom, and there was an open clothes hanger, twisted and with sharp edges. I knew right away that she might have been trying to abort her pregnancy herself.

I asked her, "Ma'am, did you use this hanger on yourself?"

She said yes.

Jimmy said, "Let's get her on the stretcher and get her in the unit."

She was still bleeding and was very weak from her loss of blood. We had just lifted her in the unit, and she started screaming. I looked between her legs, and I saw two little legs coming out.

I yelled out to Jimmy and said, "We have a breech birth!"

Jimmy went to get me the OB kit. It had the clips, scrabble, bubble syringe, pads to place under her, and solution for cleaning off the baby a little. I prepped her and had her all ready for delivery.

Right then, she had another contraction, and the baby's little body came out up to her shoulders. I had everything I needed—the pad beside me, the syringe bubble, the scalpel, the clips, and the solution. My hope was that she was dilated enough so the baby's head would be able to fit through the birth canal.

Just then, the woman had another contraction, and the baby's shoulders cleared. I could see the baby was having trouble because her mother's dilation was not the size that it needed to be. I thought to myself, *Bill, remember what you learned in the medical school.* I had to go in from underneath with my hand and feel for the baby's face. The baby's face was facing down. With my fingers, I had to feel for the baby's mouth. Once I found it, I stuck the tip of my finger inside and lowered my hand down so that the baby's head was in a lower position; it would make the diameter of the head smaller so the baby would fit through the birth canal.

During the woman's next contraction, the baby rode right out on my arm. I took the bubble syringe to suction out the fluid from the baby's mouth so she would have a better chance to breathe. A couple of seconds later, the baby finally took a breath on her own and cried. But I could see that the baby's breathing was labored.

Right then, the mother started hemorrhaging. I took the clips and arranged them on the umbilical cord and cut in between the two clips. I wrapped the baby up in my arms, and I implored Jimmy and one of the police officers that was at the scene to try to stop the hemorrhaging in the mother. I jumped into the police car with the baby and the other of the two police officers. We were only three minutes from James Mattson Hospital.

He drove fast, siren on so that we could get there as fast as possible. I held the baby in one arm and tried to brace myself with the other, and I could see the other officer was nervous. His hands were shaking on the steering wheel. Something scared me just then. We were coming to a full stop in front of the hospital, and I was holding my hand out, looking at it—it was straight as an arrow and steady as a cargo ship. I realized that, through the years, I was becoming immune to all of this. The horrifying scenes, the blood all over the bathroom floor, the heads through windshields, the dying baby in my arms. No human being should have a steady hand when going through this. My realization was cut short when we fully stopped.

We went right into the emergency room. They put the baby on a gurney, and the nurses and doctor were trying to help the baby breathe better by giving her some oxygen. The baby was premature by three months and was very, very small. Her little head was the same size as her entire body.

Just then, one of the hospital administrators came into the room and said that we had to transport the baby to Kingston Memorial Hospital. I said desperately, "The baby can't be transported. She's not stable!"

The administrator said, "She has to go. There's a helicopter on the way here to pick her up."

The helicopter landed right in front of the hospital. They brought down an incubator, with the cord sticking out of it, to plug in the wall.

I said, "This is an electrical incubator. We need a portable incubator!"

The doctors and the nurse agreed with me.

The administrator said, "You have to put the baby in here. We have no portable incubators."

"The baby can't even breathe on her own!" I yelled angrily.

The administration lady just turned and walked away. I looked at the doctors and the nurses, and I said anxiously, "How will this work?"

"Well," they said, "maybe we could put some warm pads in with her."

"How will the baby have oxygen?" I asked.

"She'll have to breathe on her own," they said.

"You see how labored the baby is still. She's not stable!" I said. I looked at one of the nurses, and I saw a tear rolling down her face.

"What kind of hospital is this!?" I yelled. I looked at the police officer and told him that maybe he could help me try to strap the incubator on the helicopter. It wasn't even a medical helicopter; it was just the regular bubble police chopper. We strapped the baby as quickly as we could onto the railing, and I jumped into the chopper with the pilot. The pilot looked at me and asked me what I weighed. I told him about 175.

"We should be all right," he said.

"Then let's go!" I shouted.

I could see the baby. She was tied on right underneath me. She was still breathing and moving a bit as we took off. I asked the pilot how long it would take to get to Kingston, and he said, "Once we were in the air, it should only take about eight minutes."

I stood there in-flight, totally helpless, and watched the baby take her last breath about six minutes into the flight. We had two minutes before we landed. We landed on the helipad at Kingston Memorial Hospital, and there was a crew of doctors and nurses standing by. When helicopter landed safely, they unstrapped the incubator, lifted it up, and put it on a gurney. The one doctor pulled the lid up and put the stethoscope on the baby's chest. "DOA," he said after a few seconds of listening.

"DOA?! Try to revive the baby! She was breathing two minutes ago!"

The doctor ignored me, turned around, and began walking back to the hospital. I started running alongside him, screaming at him. "What kind of doctor are you!? You call yourself a doctor, why don't you try to help this baby?"

One of the nurses grabbed my arm. I knew a lot of nurses at Kingston, but I didn't know this one. She asked my name, and I told her.

She said, "Bill, the baby was too premature. She wouldn't have made it."

"How do we know that?!" I implored with tears rolling down my face. It seemed like me and the one police officer were the only ones concerned about trying to keep this child alive.

We made our way inside the hospital, and a lady walked up to me and told me, "You have a phone call. Come with me."

I picked up the phone, and it was Roy, one of my bosses down at work. He told me they were sending a unit to pick me up. He told me to go out the back of the hospital and that they would pick me up there. By this time, all the news stations were lined up in front of the hospital, waiting to find out what happened with the baby that flew in on the helicopter. My company and neither of the hospitals I went to that day didn't want me talking to them, so they basically told me over the phone that if I wanted to keep my job, I would go out the back door and not say a word to the news crew.

That day, I lost a lot of respect that I once had for our medical field's administration. It was all politics—no one wanted to be responsible for that child.

"For I know the plans I have for you," declares the Lord.
"Plans to prosper and not to harm you. Plans
to give you hope and a future."

—Jeremiah 29:11 (NIV)

CHAPTER 8

Exhausted, Mentally and Physically—PTSD

Several years had passed. Being a paramedic was physically and mentally taking a toll on me. In between the years 1968 and 1980, there were thirteen riots in Miami—two big ones. One happened in 1968 before I lived there, and the other big one was in 1980 with over 1,000 National Guard troops on hand. It was crazy. The city was literally on fire. I'll never forget transporting a victim of a shooting from the cocaine wars, flying into Kingston Memorial Hospital in a medical helicopter. I was looking down at the same time, watching the whole city burn. I had never seen anything like this. We were working double shifts—sometimes seventy-two hours straight, getting very little sleep, and sometimes even getting shot at in the rescue unit.

My son, Joey, was born on August 17, 1977—on the same day that Elvis Presley died. The job also took a toll on my marriage with Angela. We were divorced in 1980. I was out, partying a lot with my friends. Our divorce was all my fault. I guess I was just somewhat young and dumb still.

One night, we were stationed at Saint John's Hospital on Miami Beach. I remember that we were not eating or sleeping—run after run after run. We had a 341 call on Seventy-ninth Street and Collins

Avenue. We arrived at the apartment, and the man had just gone into cardiac arrest. I was on the floor beside him, doing CPR on him. The next thing I knew was that I opened my eyes, and I had an IV in my arm, and I was in another rescue unit on the stretcher, being taken to Saint John's Hospital.

"How long has I passed out?"

The paramedic helping me said that I must have been out for at least twenty minutes. It must have been so bad that, once I arrived at the hospital, they had a priest there, saying a blessing over me as they took me in the ER.

The doctor was hooking me up with an IV of intravenous D5W. Without getting into medical terms, it's basically a sugar-and-water solution with electrolytes. It's used to treat low blood sugar. We weren't eating properly on the job, so that was a big possible factor as to why I had passed out. I was also severely dehydrated, and I might have had insulin shock.

I stayed in the hospital for three days, getting all kinds of tests and blood work done; my heart was fine, my kidney function came back fine, liver was good, all the blood tests came back good, so we still had to find out why I passed out. They set up one more test for me with my private doctor: a glucose tolerance test. I had to be in his office three days later. They also told me I could not return to work yet.

That Friday came quickly. I went for the test, and it was to last four hours. They drew my blood every thirty minutes. I went in after fasting, then they made you drink a bottle of glue Coke, basically just Coca-Cola syrup, at the third hour. I was sitting there in a pool of sweat, feeling terrible. The nurse asked me if I thought I could continue, as we had a whole other hour of the test. I said I wanted to continue. I almost fainted, but I made it.

After the test, they gave me some food to eat and a soda to drink. After a bit of a wait, we got the results back on my blood sugar test. At the end of the third hour, my blood sugar measured in at twenty-five. My doctor told me that he didn't know how I was even standing because the normal blood sugar level is about eighty-five to ninety-five.

After we had all the results back, I found out at my next appointment that I had chronically very low blood sugar. That night, my doctor called me into his office and advised me to take a furlough from work. After years of dealing with all the bad accidents—the gunshots, the heart attacks, and things like that lady trying to abort herself, the riots, people shooting at us while we tried to pick up the sick, all the hurt people—my body was suffering.

My doctor said to me, "Billy, all you get to see is the dark side of the medical field. If you are a nurse or a doctor, you get to see them get better. You see the positive outcome. You need that." He said, "I can see that you care and that you're sensitive."

I knew exactly what he meant. I was not like all the folks I worked with. For some of them, what they saw didn't affect them at all. They were able to compartmentalize work versus real life, but it seemed like they had no emotions. My friends at work used to tell me, "Billy, stop bringing your work home." Like after attending at a bad accident, I would think about it a lot. The only way I got relief from it was to go out partying and drinking in the clubs. It was 1980 now. I took off work for a while to rest according to the doctor's orders.

Nowadays, they have a name for what I was experiencing—PTSD.

The Lord replied, "My presence will go with you, and give you rest"

—Exodus 33:14 (NIV)

CHAPTER 9

I Became a Merchant. Prophecy? Or Coincidence?

After taking off work for a couple of months, I felt rested. I was about ready to go back. One Friday night before I started back, I was at my friend Joe's house for our regular weekly poker game that I would show up to every now and then. During our break, we were having some sodas, some beers, and we had a pizza to share. Joe wanted to show me something that he had bought.

A few months before this, Joe had actually left the rescue team to become a Teamsters truck driver; he was a part of the union and was driving big rigs and making deliveries. I guess the pay was better. At one of the places he delivered to, the owner asked him if he was interested in purchasing three large boxes of custom jewelry that were seconds. Seconds meant that they had an imperfection, so they could not be sold to stores. To the naked eye, there was nothing wrong with them though.

Inside the beautiful small, blue velvet boxes, there were beautiful gold chain sets, bracelets, necklaces, and earrings for the ladies.

Joe asked me, "What do you think we could do with these two big boxes of jewelry?"

There must have been three hundred small boxes inside each large box.

I said, "Well, I'm not doing anything now, why don't I take them out to our swap shop in Fort Lauderdale? I'll have some fun with them. I'll set them up, and maybe I'll sell a few."

Well, that next day, I went down to the office at the swap shop and reserved a spot for the weekend. I went ahead and got two eight-foot-long tables, a couple of black tablecloths, and an E-Z UP tent and began setting up. All I did was open the small boxes up, put a sign out that said, "Any box you like, pick it out. $10.00." All the jewelry boxes had tags saying $49, $59. I was selling all of them at $10.

By Sunday afternoon, I had taken in $2,800 on the two big boxes that cost me $50 each. *Amazing*, I thought. I had another box at Nick's house for the next weekend.

During the week after the swap, I contacted some big jewelry manufacturers and had samples sent to me. I created a corporation and went to get a tax ID license. This was 1980. I couldn't make $2,800 in the whole month, working as a paramedic. I was glad I was up in the card game last Friday night because I used the $100 that I won to buy the two boxes.

Suddenly, the memory of the night in 1973, when I was driving the taxi, came back to me. When Nigel came over to the window before he left, I heard him say, "Billy, remember what I told you over dinner?" Of course I did. He had said that I was going to be a merchant someday, that I would travel and buy and sell goods all over the world. I instantly got the chills, thinking, *Was Nigel sent to me to direct me toward the path God wanted me on?*

When I went back to my apartment that night, I called my mother up and told her about my weekend. I told her about how all the ladies went crazy over the jewelry boxes at the swap shop; it got so crowded that I could hardly believe it. I told her about how I had enough jewelry for next weekend and how I planned on hiring some new manufacturers. We talked for a long time that night. If anything came from that call, it was that I realized that those boxes didn't sell themselves. I had a talent for sales.

After we hung up, I was thinking about growing up in Brooklyn. When I was a little boy, my mother owned a bar and grill across the street from Ebbets Field, where the Brooklyn Dodgers played. She owned the bar from the early 1940s until the late 1960s. My mother's name was Olga, a Ukrainian lady. She was a coal miner's daughter from Taylor, Pennsylvania.

My mom was a great cook. On game days, she brought me into work with her because she had box seats right behind home plate. She had signed pictures of all the Dodgers on all her walls in the bar. I remember names like Leo Durocher (the manager), Gil Hodges, Pee Wee Reese, Roy Campanella, Jackie Robinson—so many photos.

One day, she told me that Leo brought in a young man in for lunch. Leo said to her, "Olga, give the young man a Coca-Cola with his lunch. He's too young to have a beer with us."

Mom asked the young man for his name, and he replied, "Sandy Koufax, ma'am. I hope to be a great ballplayer one day."

It was a sad day in 1957 when the Dodgers announced they were leaving Brooklyn and moving to Los Angeles.

My dad was the president of Teamsters Union Local 804. Dad brought United Parcel Service into the Teamsters Union in 1940. I remember that one big convention that Dad went to every year was in Miami Beach. He told me all about the beautiful beaches and the palm trees. He also told me about a big fishing trip that he went on with Jimmy Hoffa, the president of all the Teamsters locals. Dad and Jimmy were friends.

My dad had a good heart. Whenever I asked him to help with one of my friends that was heading in the wrong direction, he would get them a job on the trucks. They made good money, and it kept them off the streets and out of trouble. He taught me about trust, loyalty, and respect. And those three words, I will never forget.

Fast forward to March 1963. I was in my classroom at school when it came over our loudspeaker that President John F. Kennedy was shot in Dallas. I went home from school that day, and Mom and

Christine were sitting at the kitchen table, crying. Christine helped raise me while Mom was at the bar cooking.

In our house, there was always singing going on all the time. My mother sang with some of the biggest bands at that time. She even sang once with the Tommy Dorsey band. And may I say, she was one beautiful lady. Christine sang so beautifully. She had a voice that was fit for the blues, just like Diana Ross. There were singers all around our neighborhood in Brooklyn, like the Tokens and Vito & The Salutations. One of my neighbors that lived at 460 Ocean Parkway (we lived at 490) was a lady by the name of Barbra Streisand. It's too bad I never got to meet her. I became a singer myself once upon a time. I landed the lead role in our play at school. I played Tony in *West Side Story*.

There I was, years after the JFK assassination, I came home that day and found Mom and Christine at the kitchen table, crying. I asked them what happened, and they told me that Martin Luther King Jr. had been shot. That was a sad day for all humanity.

I went down to the draft board to register when I became eighteen. Later that night, when I went home, I told my mom that I was excited to get my draft card. That same night, I heard my mom yelling at my dad, saying, "Joe, don't let my boy go to Vietnam." She said. "I can't take another son's death."

My older brother, Peter, had just passed away from cancer. I never heard from the draft board. I really don't know what happened, but I guess that my dad had some very important friends.

Around that time, I got my driver's license. One of the men from the neighborhood bar approached me. This particular bar was always filled with mob guys. Outside the bar, there were nothing but Cadillacs and Lincolns.

My group of friends would hang out across the street. We used to sing beautiful songs in four-part harmony. People would walk by and stop to listen. If we were lucky, they would throw some money in the hat for us, and by the end of the night, we usually wound up with some good change.

I actually knew the man that had approached me. His name was Louie. They all had nicknames, like Louie the Lip, Joey Bag of

Donuts—you name it. They were all funny names. Louie came up to me, handed me $300 and a set of keys to a brand-new Cadillac Eldorado that was supposedly parked on E Eighth Street. He told me to drive it across town and drop it off at some body shop chop shop. I turned to him, handed him the keys and the $300 back, and said, "No, thank you."

He said, "You're Joe Tortorella's boy, aren't you?"

After I replied yes, he said nervously, "Say hello to your dad for me. And do me a favor, don't say anything to him about the car thing." *Car thing,* as he phrased it.

I had other plans for my life than becoming a mobster, and they were across the Brooklyn Bridge. I was about to graduate from the school of art and design, and I had a good job lined up with a big advertising agency. Back in those days, Brooklyn was exactly like the movies.

CHAPTER 10

February 1994, Tucson, Arizona My Near-death Experience

I owned two jewelry shops: one in Fort Lauderdale and one in Pompano Beach, both were in Florida. I was working at a trade show in Tucson, Arizona, in February 1994. I had already done three shows in January, and just the week before, I was at another show in Santa Monica, California.

This show in Tucson though was one of our best shows of the year. It was a fourteen-day trade show that was also open to the public. People would attend the show from all over the world, as it happened to be the biggest gem and jewelry show on the planet. Believe it or not, the whole city was a show. The convention center was filled, all the hotel ballrooms filled, every hotel room booked. Some of the hotel rooms even had vendors in them, and they would sell right out of their rooms.

I had a big watch business, about 700 different styles of watches in my line. I also sold sterling silver jewelry. A lot of silver from Bali in David Yurman and John Hardy styles, semiprecious stones in a lot of beautiful styles, some fourteen-karat gold products, cubic zirconia rings, and tennis bracelets for the ladies.

The whole city, like I said, was always booming with dealers at the Tucson show. It was exciting to be able to meet people and deal with folks from all over the world. My company had set up a big double booth at the Holidome at the Holiday Inn in Tucson. The third day into the show, we were doing very well.

Unfortunately, a lot of people were getting sick and falling very ill around us. A horrible virus broke out, and it seemed like everyone was getting sick. At that time, it was a virus that the health officials couldn't identify, and we were worried it might be something like the hantavirus.

Four days into the show, I became extremely ill, so bad that I couldn't even work our booth. Luckily, by this time, I had other people working for me. My throat was so sore and swollen that I could hardly breathe, and I had a high fever. I was so weak from the virus, and I also had a severe case of sleep apnea that I wasn't aware of. The next day, it was so bad that I went to the medical clinic, where they gave me some antibiotics and an inhaler to help me breathe. They told me to go to the hospital in the morning if it didn't get any better, so I went back to my hotel room, and all I could do was try to rest.

CHAPTER 11

My NDE—My Near-death Experience

My miserable day turned into a night of light and love. During the night, my sleep apnea and the virus just closed my throat down, and I stopped breathing.

I remember it vividly, even today. I departed from my body through my eyes in this beautiful, glowing green, fluorescent mist; it was the color of life. The green color was somehow magnified hundreds of times; it was magnificent. They say the eyes are the windows of our soul—maybe this is the reason for our departure from our body through them.

Now I was hovering over my body on my bed, and I looked down upon myself. How cumbersome that body appeared. It looks lifeless. I was so happy to be free. The feeling of freedom and lightness overwhelmed me. I strangely felt so relieved, so relieved to be out of it. I turned and saw a gateway—a beautiful tunnel of light and love opened. That's the only way I can describe it—that I was part of the light and love, drawn to its beauty.

What was amazing about the tunnel was that it was made up of beautiful colors that you could have never imagined when alive—it seemed that all these colors were magnified. It was like when you hold a prism to the sun and the colors just dazzle you. They were the most stunning reds, violets, blues, greens, yellows. I was entranced and felt pulled toward the light.

I felt as if I started moving faster and faster until I felt like I was traveling at the speed of light. The colors were moving by me and through me. During all of this, I was not afraid. I felt nothing but protection and love, as if I had come through this gateway before. The light and love felt as if it was growing stronger and stronger. I felt welcomed, and this feeling of love both overcame and became me. I was traveling home, and I was arriving where I was supposed to be.

I was in a vast and open, illuminated area. It was absolutely magnificent. I could see other spirits around me. They were welcoming me. "We have been awaiting your arrival," I heard a sweet voice say behind me.

I turned and saw another amazingly beautiful and breathtaking spirit. She approached me and said in her soft, warm voice, "My name is Antonia. I am your travel guardian. I have been traveling with you home, Bill."

"Home," I said, "I'm finally home! Thank God I'm home, back in the light of my Lord Jesus Christ, my God!" I was absolutely ecstatic.

Antonia said, "Yes, Bill, you're home." "All these beautiful glowing spirits are your family and friends," she said.

I was looking at them, and we were communicating together. It was so wonderful hearing, not in voices but with a kind of telepathy. I heard every word they were saying. I couldn't help but say it again, "I'm home!" And I was home. I've been here before, and I was back. It was so joyous.

My guardian told me, "You're back in the light of our Lord Jesus."

"I know, I can feel him in the light," I said serenely.

"Jesus is the light, and the light is his love, wisdom, and knowledge," she said.

I was totally immersed in the light of God and my Lord Jesus Christ. My spirit was relaxed. I couldn't remember my life on earth anymore. I didn't even want to remember. All I felt was love. This love was different. It was something you can't explain, standing here in my spirit circle, communicating with friends and family from the other side. I was being bombarded with their knowledge and reasons for the meaning of life.

If I were to explain how it looks in heaven, I would describe it as a collection of magnificent crystal cities. The roads were paved with gold and diamonds. These crystal buildings reflected the light and colors of the universe. All the pictures of nebulas, clouds of stardust, planetary systems, and galaxies that you see on earth come to life in the reflections of these buildings. Bustling in and around these buildings were hundreds of thousands, if not millions, of spirits, working in service for one another. It seemed that the spirit remained pleasantly busy while in heaven.

There was no "I" or "me" when in this place. Any remaining sense of individuality melted away, and we were all one in the light of Jesus—we were in God's hands at all times. Everything was so advanced, so unconcerned with the pettiness of life on earth, so secure and united. We are all connected.

Antonia took me to a quiet area. She turned to me and said, "It's time for your life review."

I asked, "What review?"

"Your life review," she responded.

Antonia stepped back and disappeared. I turned, and my second guardian stepped in. As soon as he spoke, I knew it was my brother Peter. I haven't heard his voice since I was sixteen years old.

Peter said, "How are you, Billy?" He always called me Billy, not Bill. "Your life review is starting."

Now for the first time since leaving earth, I saw myself in my body, and I saw my life now. It was shown to me—everything good and everything bad. All the events of my life, I could feel them, and I relived them. The lessons I was supposed to have learned—the right and the wrong choices that I've made.

This was where you felt hell—it was not an eternal afterlife. I felt the pain that I put onto others as well. It put me right in their shoes, and I felt the pain that I caused to others. The pain, the sadness, the sorrow, the grief—it was all rolled up into one potent and agonizing experience. I became their pain. I felt that all the pain was too hard to accept anymore. It was the worst feeling I have ever felt in my life.

I felt myself in the shoes of all the people that I've wronged—actual, physical pain on top of the shame and sorrow that came with it.

I felt the pain that I caused my first wife, Angela, and our son, Joey. The pain that I caused when I left them. There was no excuse for my selfishness back then. In this moment, all I could hope was that I've made it up to Joey over the years. God knew I had tried.

The experience was just becoming too much to handle now. I couldn't imagine what people, who have lived more selfish lives than I had, would experience in their life reviews. My heavenly body, for the first time, felt heavy, almost too heavy to stay standing. It was harrowing to have to experience every wrongdoing you have ever committed all in one go, and I started to break down. I was saying, "Please, forgive me. Forgive me! I am sorry I caused this pain!"

*For judgment is without mercy to one who has shown
no mercy. Mercy triumphs over judgment.*

—James 2:13 (ESV)

I then heard a man's voice, and it all stopped, though I didn't feel peace right away. I mean, I've just relived every hardship that I've ever caused someone on earth. I didn't see the source of the voice, but I heard him say again, "Now he will experience the good events in his life."

This life review was where you feel heaven also—everything good you've done. You will experience it again. It all came back to you, just like the bad events.

I saw myself as a child, sharing with my friends.

I was a very lucky boy. My mom and dad always did all right for themselves with my dad being the president of 804 Teamsters local and my mom owning her bar and grill. When my mom gave me some money for something like ice cream or for the movies, I would always pay for my friends because their families didn't have it to give.

Some of my friends went down the wrong road when we were teenagers. A lot of them started taking heroin and shooting up. I remember trying to save my good friend Donny. I had to get him out of one of the worst areas and buildings in Brooklyn's neighborhoods. I was walking up the staircase, trying not to step on people that were lying all over the hallways, all drugged out, some of them with needles still hanging out of their arms. I finally found him on the fourth floor, slumped over in the back of a dirty, rat-infested apartment building that night. I had to get him out of there, so I put my arms under his, picked him up, and started dragging him out down the hallway. A couple of the junkies started yelling at me. I told them to shut up and sit back down. It wasn't any of their business.

I wasn't worried about them jumping me too much; they were all so stoned that they could hardly stand. Donny had lost so much weight that I was able to pick him up and put him over my shoulder. I got him down to the car, and he confusedly took a swing at me. I just grabbed him and shook him a little to knock some sense into him, and he fell to the ground. I picked him back up and put him in the back seat. I drove him home to his mother's house.

"Mrs. Rotella, we have to get him help!" I announced when I got inside.

It was terrible. He was my best friend. By the time I was seventeen years old, I must have been to ten funerals—all from drug overdoses. I tried to be there for all the families that was going through so much grief.

Peter showed me all the times when I was a paramedic in Miami, working on people—on John, bringing him back to life after being dead quite a while; the accident when Carol's head went through the windshield, calling out to God for help, feeling that strong need to go back to Pine's General Hospital the next day. They were showing me so much more. When we picked up the lady that tried to abort herself, how hard we worked to keep that baby alive. I heard a voice say, "You did well, Bill."

Thank God the good outweighed the bad. A cloud of gray disappeared, and I was back in my spirit form in a spectacular, illuminated light.

Peter, my guardian and brother, was by my side on earth the whole time. When I called out for God's help, he was the one directing me and helping me. Peter was the one who guided my finger in the baby's mouth when the mother had her breech birth. I was so fortunate I had him as a guide during my life on earth.

Peter then explained that I had three guardians that were with me my whole life on earth.

"My guardian angels!" I said in response.

He smiled and said, "Yes, we all try to achieve the status of angels from our Lord Jesus."

Peter told me that the baby I tried my heart out to save was here and was part of my spirit circle. I was so happy to hear that. I felt tears rolling down my face. I asked Peter who my third guardian was.

"He's a great old spirit. Thousands of years old. One of God's greatest angels. Oron is his name. He's your guardian of knowledge, wisdom, and intuition. He's the angel that sits on your shoulder and speaks to you through intuition and leads you down the right path. But God doesn't allow him to stop you from making your choices, whether right or wrong. You make your own path."

Peter said to me that my mission on earth was to learn—feelings of pain, guilt, laughter, happiness, grief, love, sorrow. He said, "But your service is the most important lesson of your life—the more you give of yourself in service by helping to give in a form of an action, not just in the form of money. Service is an action in itself, transferring love to one another and caring."

Great servants of God, like Mother Teresa, are saints in his eyes. When she was still on earth, Mother Teresa found a woman dying on the steps of the church in Kolkata, and she stood with the woman until she passed. She then dedicated the rest of her life to the poorest people in India and went on to win the Nobel Prize. Think of Gandhi. He preached nonviolence as the greatest weapon of mankind. He believed that nonviolence could change the world. He earned the name Mahatma Gandhi, meaning "great soul." Think of a lady by the name of Maria Espinoza. She built the Betania shrine in Venezuela; how many healings and miracles took place there? Maria is well-known. She was visited by the mother Mary when she was very young, and she has been changing and saving many lives through the power of miracles. These people were God's angels on earth.

Peter said, "We are your three guardians. Antonia is your travel guardian. She takes you in, and she also takes you home. I'm your guardian sent from God when you call on him for help. Oron, the old angel of wisdom, is your guardian of knowledge and intuition."

Suddenly, an angel, a master of knowledge came forward. He glowed with a magnificent light, and I could feel as he approached that he was a great spirit. I felt his wisdom like he has been with me my entire life. I should have felt intimidated, and maybe even a bit afraid, of the powerful being standing just a few feet away, but I didn't. I felt comforted, like I was in the presence of an old friend.

Peter said, "Welcome, Oron."

Oron approached me and said, "Bill, we are going on to the next level."

We were suddenly in human form once again. I felt and looked somewhat younger, maybe early in my early thirties. Oron looked to me only about forty years old, despite his having lived for several thousands of years. I asked, "Oron, don't you age here in heaven?"

He responded, "In the light of our Lord, we're only in human form at certain levels of enlightenment."

We were standing in a grand theater, enormous in size. Oron said to me that this was the hall of events. What I witnessed next was nothing short of amazing. A giant screen opened in front of us, but we were somehow a part of every scene with clips of what looked to me like newsreels flickering at incredible speed. It stopped and went. It transported me and Oron from clip to clip, and it felt like we were in every scene.

I was being transported back to the scene with me in the rescue unit in Miami on the way to the hospital, pleading with God to help me. In this scene though, I could see Peter right beside me, helping me stop the bleeding from Carol's head. Then suddenly, it transported us to another event, and the next thing I knew, I was being taken to that apartment where the young lady aborted herself with a clothes hanger. Once again, I could see Peter with me, helping me direct my hands and fingers to find the baby's mouth to help me move the baby's head in the right position. Just like that, we were moving in time again to my collapse when I was doing CPR on the man that had just gone into cardiac arrest. I was watching myself be taken into another rescue unit, opening my eyes, and asking the medic how long I had been out for.

All three guardians were with me now. I felt like Jesus was speaking to me through them. They were the Holy Trinity. They all stood with me.

Oron said, "Bill, we knew you had, had enough, seeing terrible car accidents, heart attacks, strokes, and shootings every single day. Your mind has just had enough, and you need time to heal yourself. Your drinking and partying just took a toll on you as well."

"Any person with any kind of feeling for mankind should never have had to do what you did for that long," Antonia said to me.

"I know I was a wreck for some time," I said.

Again, out of nowhere, I was moving through time. This time, I was in Bangkok, Thailand, on my trip to both vacation and to buy inventory for my business. As soon as we arrived at the airport at that time, I felt like someone was in my ear—now I knew. *Thank you, Oron.* Now I knew better. He was warning me when we were taken by those corrupt military police. I knew they were going to try to kill me.

Peter said, "I had to step in and help your tour guide get the nerve to stand up to them."

I said, "Peter, I don't know what you did to her to give her that kind of nerve."

We were moving forward again, faster and faster. Years were going by, but we kept moving. This time, we passed my death. When we stopped, it was September 11, 2001, and we were at the base of the Twin Towers. People were starting to run, there was ash everywhere, and I had friends working in the first tower that went down. I started running away, and Peter said, "Bill, stop. You don't have to run. Remember, this hasn't happened yet."

And now, the tower was coming down all around us. I didn't feel anything, not even the debris.

We were moving again but stopped abruptly. I was in my mother-in-law's home in Pennsylvania with my wife Kristen. Kristen and I met in 1991. It was instantly that I knew she was the woman I had been waiting for my entire life. One year before, in 1990, I completed an oil painting of a woman walking down from a mountain. When we met, Kristen had just moved to Fort Lauderdale from the Pocono Mountains in Pennsylvania, and she looked exactly like the woman in my painting.

Now in this living room, I was watching Kristen and her mother, seeing what we now know as the worst and deadliest terrorist attack in American history live on TV. I turned to them and said, "Another plane is coming."

No response. I yelled out again, panicked, "Another plane is coming!"

"They can't hear you," Peter said. "Remember, this is your future."

We were moving yet again with no warning and no closure from what I just witnessed, and we stopped. There were bombs coming down all around us. I looked around, and again, people were running. I thought this was Baghdad. They were going after Saddam Hussein. I somehow knew what was going on, yet this had never happened on earth.

I was continuing to move through these events—some important for the entire world, some important for just myself, like flickering newsreels for what seemed like forever, and then it stopped. Everything stopped and was quiet again. I was back in the presence of my guardians in the grand theater in the center of the magnificent crystal city. After all I had just seen, I felt something I had never felt before. It was not quite the relief I was expecting to feel after something like that. There was a hint of anxiety since Oron had said to me that the things that I had witnessed were all going to happen. Frankly, I was overwhelmed, particularly by the events in the future. There were some things that I was shown that I knew I would always hold on to because they involved future choices that still could be made.

"These are only some of the events of your future," Peter told me.

And just like that, the hall of events has vanished. Me and my guardians were standing together. All three guardians—Antonia, Peter, and Oron—brought me up to a level of amazing enlightenment, and now, I was standing in front of a huge panel of guardian angels. They seemed so advanced. There was an abundant amount of love and knowledge with this group of angels. All the answers of mankind and the universe all fell within my reach. I was taking in mass amounts of wisdom just by standing there. One of the angels began to approach me, and as he got closer, I felt more and more immersed as more information poured in about, strangely, numbers. The guardian angel began explaining a sequence of events linked to my life.

I distinctly saw my set of numbers that would alert me to many events of my lifetime. This amazed me. My set of numbers was sixty-six. I already had, had events in my life related to these numbers, whether they be good events or bad ones. They were my own personal signal from my guardians. Sometimes in one day, I would see these numbers at every glance. I would look at the clock—6:06. I looked down at my speedometer, and I was driving sixty-six mph. I looked up, and I was at Exit 66. I felt this was not just for me.

Peter told me that music and numbers were a big part of their communication throughout the heavens. During all this time, I was still being bombarded with information and wisdom.

Oron said, "Your life path number is three—that represents the Holy Trinity. And something about the number nine, being the strongest number in the universe!"

All of this was beyond my comprehension at that time. Pay close attention to your intuition, and all these wonderful new thoughts were placed in my mind by God's angels, who all lived in the full light of our Lord Jesus Christ.

Be aware of your number sequence. A lot of you have them but may or may not recognize it. The number events are strong alerts from our spirit guides. We must pay attention to our intuition; our lives are set with a path that we must follow.

Being encircled by this glorious guardian angels of knowledge and love, I now called them my guardian angels of enlightenment. My spirit was being gifted all the answers of the universe—so many that it was impossible to take it all in at once. This immense knowledge and wisdom was fuel for my soul. I felt more alive now than I ever did on earth. My teachers overwhelmed me with messages of love. It was here that I received the nine principle of enlightenment and was told that these principles were my gifts from them.

All too quickly, the most beautiful of the angels that I have yet seen walked up to me. I was taken aback by her sheer beauty. It was like nothing I had ever seen. She then told me that I must return to earth.

What? Why me? I'm home! Why do I have to go back? All these thoughts raced through my mind. I was taken aback and incredibly disappointed, more than when I wasn't able to do the interview on TV because the video team was diverted from New York City all those years ago. Despite this, I couldn't help but feel like something wasn't quite complete.

She approached again and said to me, "Dad, I am six of six, you must return."

I was so desperately pleading to stay that the Dad thing went right over my head. I said, "For goodness' sake, I'm in the light of God our Lord Jesus. The most wonderful feeling of my life. I'm one with love! And they want to send me back!?"

The angel said, "You have all the knowledge, and you must pass it on. You're the messenger."

Then it hit me. She said *Dad.*

I said, "Dad? What do you mean?"

Without any warning, I was being pulled away from everything. My heavenly body was being sucked through a vortex at an incredible speed. This time, it wasn't nearly as comforting or exciting. The colors seemed duller. I felt fear for the first time since escaping from my human body. I feel out of control. My body limped like a rag doll as I was making the journey back to earth, flawed and vulnerable.

The next thing I knew, I was back in my body, full of pain. I was gasping for air, yet I couldn't move my body. It felt like it was paralyzed. Slowly, my blood started moving through my body to my arms and hands and legs. I finally got some sensation back. I slowly reached for the phone and called the operator for help to take me to the hospital.

When I arrived at the hospital, they said that my oxygen levels were extremely low, so they put me on oxygen and monitored my blood pressure and pulse. At this time, I was still very ill, and I was afraid to say anything at that time to the doctors in the hospital about what happened to me in that hotel room.

CHAPTER 12

The Night of Light and Love

I can still remember the night of light and love. I could divide my life into two distinct sections: before my near-death experience and after.

My life was altered dramatically by my meeting with the beautiful spirits and my three guardian angels. It was at this time that the nine principals of enlightenment were revealed to me. It was now 2003. It had taken years for me to be brave enough to tell my story, but what a story it is. It's time to talk about both the Princples of enlightenment and of universal wisdom that were unveiled to me on that night that changed my life. It's my belief that they could change your life as well. I have faith they could change the world. These truths are surprisingly simple and straightforward.

Knowledge is simply remembering what we have forgotten. I call on you to read and remember, as I was called on to pass this knowledge on to you.

The last angel that I spoke with said to me that when I returned, there would be much work to be done.

Death is not an end—it's a new beginning. It's your gateway through to eternity.

We are living in troubling times. After 9/11, our country launched a war with Al-Qaeda, Iraq, and other countries. It's now twenty years later, and major problems are still going on in that region of the world. The stock markets are crazy. They've been going up and up and up, but any day, it could crash when we are not ready for it. It seems like huge corporations are running everything.

It's 2021 now. People are losing faith in the nation's future. This new world we live in with COVID-19 is becoming divided and broken up. Russia has just invaded the Ukraine. These are warnings that things need to change. This is the time to make choices that can change the outcome of our world. If we are unwilling to change our current methodology, it will bring us to total devastation and distraction. There is a positive and negative energy that has endured throughout the ages. Living with the fear, violence, and hate that exist today is living on the dark side. Our society is residing in a negative plateau.

I will take you on a journey to a level of enlightenment. This is a place where love rules and our spirits grow and prosper. There is an abundance of love and wealth that exist here when we reach this plateau. The world changes its current direction, and all of humanity will change to the path of light, or we could lose it all. Some people consistently choose to be negative, and with social media nowadays, they can gain many followers. These are the people who will cause great harm, not only to an individual but to a whole nation of people. This is antithetical to all of God's laws. The one thing that we should know is that we can control the outcome of events. We can influence the outcome the world is taking. It is our responsibility to do so. God's laws of enlightenment are simple and easy to follow. The nine steps in heaven are our nine principles of enlightenment.

CHAPTER 13

God's Light and His Great Guardians

And my God will supply every need of yours
According to his riches in glory in Christ Jesus.

—Philippians 4:19 (ASV)

The guardians are the masters of the light. They are truly the enlightened ones, the guardians of our universe. Within them are all the answers of mankind. God fills them with the answers and the wisdom of his light. God is the light that fills us with life, and his love engulfs us all in Jesus's name.

The memory I am left with is one of complete love. I know that the time I spent in heaven with my three guardian angels of our universe has changed my life forever. I do miss it. I know where my home is here on earth and the things I must do, but I do miss it. The feeling I had when I was there could not be explained in the form that we are in here on earth. My mind has become so acute to my senses, and I embraced the gift that was given to me to convey.

The heavens are a wondrous place of beautiful spirits of light, of love. My guardians' communication with me was so wise. One of my guardian angels must have been thousands of years old. His light has filled me with the wisdom. I remember vividly the teaching of enlightenment and God's laws. The feeling I had that I was finally home was so overpowering to me that I knew I belonged there. When I was told that I had to return, it was by another spirit of my circle, a lighter spirit with softer hues but brilliant beauty—my future daughter.

I remember not wanting to return, but my life cycle was not complete yet. My son, Billy, was about to be born in September of 1994, and I had another brilliant beauty coming into my life—my daughter, Brianna. She was the spirit that sent me back here so that we could be together on earth. By the way, she was born on June 6, 2000, the sixth day of the sixth month. The number sixty-six sequence that has been repeated, at work, and impacting my life in such a beautiful way.

CHAPTER 14

Our Guides and Miracles

*F*or miracles to happen in our lives, we must believe in them and the power that comes from prayer. Prayer is our direct line to heaven.

He who seeks miracles shall find wisdom. For the ones that perform miracles are God's healers. They are the chosen ones and the messengers.

Miracles are given to us every day, so be open to them, and they will find you. Ask for them in your prayers. When we pray, we actually communicate with our guides. When we talk to God in prayer, it's our phone line into heaven.

Since my near-death experience, I have learned that my guardians assist me. They direct me and help me to make sense of my experience. I have learned that my guardians are with me and have been with me all throughout my life. They direct me and help me make decisions. They're are wonderful spirits of light that help protect me. Some may call them guardian angels. They are our sentries. These guardians were given their assignments by God. They walk with us every step of the way. They help us adjust to our circumstances and lead us down the road that we should follow. When we achieve the level of guardian, we have gained the trust of God. Guardians are God's spiritual workers. You don't have to look for a path; it will be there for you. Too much deliberation is not necessary. What should be is already written for you.

Blessed are those who believe without seeing.

—John 20:29 (NLT)

Have you ever experienced déjà vu? It's a feeling that you have when you've seen something or experience something that you believe you have seen before. Déjà vu is real. You have seen it before, and you have felt it before. Prior to entering this life, we choose the body that we inhibit. We choose a character and the circumstances. We are shown every moment of a life before we arrive. It's an adventure. We see our future unfold from the moment we arrive to the day we go home. Now, that's where freedom of choice comes. In heaven, we get our assignment, and we feel that it'll be easy, as we have all the knowledge of the universe when we are there. Once you arrive here on earth though, it's a whole new plan because we make a lot of mistakes along the way, and that's okay, as long as we correct them and bring ourselves back to the right choice. Choices can bring us down the right path or the wrong path, which can take us down a whole array of different directions. If this happens to you, listen to your intuition. Pay attention to those voices and try to stay on the right road.

When I said in heaven, "I'm home, I'm finally home," it's because your life in heaven is your home, with your guardians and your spiritual family. That is your real home. Earth is just a temporary abode. It's a school of knowledge from which we graduate. We learn our lessons, and then we can return home. And one of the most wonderful lessons I've learned is that we travel in our family's spirit circle! So our loved ones remain by our sides.

CHAPTER 15

Heaven's Zip Code

Our home is the stardust, the beautiful nebulas of our universe, like the Orion and Eagle Nebulas. Could they be the birthplace of our stars and planets? Supernovas are exploding giant stars that are dying. They form into giant nebulas that are illuminated clouds of gases and stardust. In heaven that reminds me of beautiful crystal cities with streets of gold. This is where life begins—in the magnificent, brilliant colors of its glow. This process repeats itself over and over until it creates life.

What science is not aware of is that, within these magnificent nebulas, there is life, love, knowledge, and wisdom that is so advanced. These are the enlightened ones, our guardian angels, our families, and our spirits. These glowing forms of illumination are all the creation of God's hands.

These angels are our great guardians of our past, present, and future. I experienced a communication with those beautiful angels and spirits. That experience has changed my life. It wasn't until I went to the Kennedy Space Center in May 2009 with my wife, Kristen, and children. I was looking at some of the most beautiful pictures of the Orion Nebula, taken with the Hubble Telescope. The colors were so magnificent that chills would pour through my body. It was the feeling of seeing and being there before, in my near-death experience.

What if the energy of the universe itself could think, feel love, and create? The energy with the force of life was the maker of all mankind—God himself. We know that he is the light and that he has created all of mankind.

In the beginning God created the Heavens and the earth.
Now the earth was formless and empty,
darkness was over the surface of the deep,
and the spirit of God was hovering over the water,
and God said. "Let there be light."
And there was light.

—Genesis 1 (NIV)

CHAPTER 16

My Return Home from Tucson

I made it back home from Tucson. I was back in Florida. It was March 1994. My wife, Kristen, and I had been married since 1991. I didn't know how to explain my near-death experience to her. First of all, I didn't even know what a near-death experience was in 1994. I was remembering all of those outer-body experiences in fear that no one would understand what I went through. It was incredibly isolating, knowing the secrets of the universe and feeling like I couldn't talk about it.

Back then, it wasn't talked about in regular conversations. I couldn't believe that it was still not talked about freely now in 2021, when there are hundreds of thousands of documented cases of people dying from heart attacks, dying at home, dying on an operating table or an accident, and have been revived. Tens of thousands of us have very similar stories. You would think that with all the proof out there, that the average person would be well aware of what a near-death experience is. You would think that people would pay more attention to these miracles that happen every day and they would be on a path to enlightenment. I guess until it happens to each and every individual, they will never actually know or believe.

One night after dinner, I couldn't take the loneliness and confusion anymore, and I told Kristen about my experience in Tucson, Arizona. I told her about how I left my body, how I had met my guardians, how I had seen all the events of my life on earth, past and future. I was terrified, but I couldn't take it anymore. Patiently and understandingly, she listened. When I was finished, she was completely nonjudgmental, and though she had never heard of a near-death experience either, she could see how serious I was when I explained everything to her, and she believed me. After a bit of thought, she advised me to go talk to my doctor, Dr. Vasquez.

It felt good that she didn't say anything negative about it. She wanted me to go to be able to get some answers, emphasizing that I shouldn't have to feel this way about something so amazing. I made an appointment for the following week. The appointment came, and the doctor asked me what was wrong, and I just said that it was time for a full examination, and he took me in the exam room and gave me my exam. He was taking my blood for a full workup, and I finally got the courage, and I asked him if I could speak to him about something that happened to me during the Tucson show.

He had me follow him into his office. I sat down, looking at all the diplomas on his wall. I thought about how I had been with Dr. Vazquez since I was a paramedic down in Miami years ago, and I started feeling less nervous and more comfortable talking to him. I explained to him the whole story of my near-death experience. After we finished, we sat there for about thirty or forty seconds of silence. I guess he was gathering his thoughts. I said, "I'm glad you have time for me this afternoon to talk."

"Bill, don't be nervous," he said, "You are my seventh patient that has come back from being dead and have a similar story."

What? I died and came back to life! How could this be? I thought.

He said that they all remember floating above their bodies. Two had watched the doctors working on them after they died on the operating table, both of them brought back with the defibrillator paddles. Three of the other patients that died on the way to the hospital or at home had more of an experience like mine. They were drawn to the light in the tunnel. They even used the words "I'm finally home" when they arrived in heaven. At that point, one was told that they had to return, and the other two went through their full life review, and then returned.

One patient told Dr. Vasquez everything that they did to him after he was in full cardiac arrest. He listed off the drugs given to him, word for word, as they were putting them into his body, what the doctors were saying to each other while performing CPR, how many ccs of epinephrine was shot into his heart, even the label of the lights that were used above his body—because he was above it, watching. Then he remembered entering back into his body after the third shock of the defibrillators.

I was so happy I was not alone in this world. The torment in my mind had finally eased, and I felt pure, utter relief.

Dr. Vazquez told me, "Bill, you have been blessed." He told me about the concept of a near-death experience, a term that I had never heard of before. I was both relieved and shocked to find out that others had experienced the same thing as me. I had now gone almost four years without knowing the term, thinking that I was alone, but the thought that others had experienced something so implausible was a total shock.

It was then that Dr. Vasquez asked me to go back into the examination room so that he could give me an electrocardiogram. After the test, we went back into his office after the results came out, and he said, "Just as I thought. Have you ever had a heart attack before?"

"No, never!" I said.

Then he said, "It sure looks like your heart has stopped at some point." He told me not to worry, that it looked fine now, but that he could prove that, at that one point all those years ago, I had undoubtedly died. He wanted to send me out for a sleep test. At that test, I found out that I have sleep apnea.

I remember he gave me a couple of books to read. For years, I just kept it between my wife, a couple of people in my family, and Dr. Vazquez.

The last thing Dr. Vazquez told me was, "Some people find God. But you, Bill Tortorella, you were blessed and got to meet God."

CHAPTER 17

The Nine Principles of Enlightenment

Simplicity reigns supreme and simplicity will save us. Nourishment and growth of the soul is directly correlated to the adherence to these basic universal principles.

First Principle: You will not and should not take the life of anyone, including yourself. There are no exceptions. It is wrong to change an individual's path or direction. This can change destiny. You can change the outcome of our whole future. However, you do have the right to protect yourself in self-defense.

Second Principle: The warnings and your intuition. Listen to the warnings. These are signs that manifest as intuition. Learn and listen, and respect those voices.

Third Principle: Choices. God gives us the power of choice. Right or wrong, good or bad—it's ours to make. All choices have an outcome that we must live with.

Fourth Principle: Give of yourself through service. Your services are needed in a form of action, not money.

Fifth Principle: Ask God to enlarge your wealth, and he will enlarge your spirit.

Sixth Principle: Seek the lessons. Lessons are sent to us to help us expand on territories and open new doors.

Seventh Principle: Unleash the power of love. When you do this, you get a taste of what the spirit world is like. You feel the warmth, love, and peace in your soul.

Eighth Principle: The body is a temple. Your body is your vessel that you sail from birth to passage. Keep it from harm.

Ninth Principle: Protect Mother Earth. She is the birth mother of humanity. The earth does not belong to us. We belong to her, and she is the force that connects us all. There is only one race, and that is the human race.

When we harness the nine principle s of enlightenment,
We are one with the light and with the love of God.
There are levels of ascension as well.
The first level is separation—the spirit leaving the body.
The second level—the spirit hovering over the body, looking down upon it, making sure the body is lifeless.
The third level—the spirit is drawn to the gateway, a tunnel of light.
The fourth level—the spirit travels at magnificent speeds.
The fifth level—arrival. The spirit understands it is home, that it has entered into the light of God.
The sixth level—the spirit meets with their guardians and other family members.
The seventh level—the spirit experiences their life review.
The eighth level—the hall of events. The spirit witnesses past, present, and future events.
The ninth level—the spirit is bombarded with knowledge, wisdom, and the nine principle s of enlightenment.

For the gate is narrow and the way is hard
that leads to life, and those who find it are few.

—Matthew 7:14 (ESV)

CHAPTER 18

The First Principle of Enlightenment— The Taking of a Life

During my near-death experience, I was gifted with of a plethora of messages from my guardians. These wonderful guardians of light, with so much love and so much knowledge, expressed to me so much enlightenment. The messages were so clear that they were placed in my soul—messages of choice and intuition that will stay with me for all eternity.

The first message I have is that we must not interfere with one's path or destiny—meaning, taking someone's life, someone's spiritual path but especially our own. We are on a course of learning and achievement of our life cycle. This process brings us to another level in heaven. We choose our life on earth before we arrive. That's why we receive our intuitions with the help from our guardians, and depending on how intuitive we are, we can experience a life déjà vu.

There are no exceptions. It is wrong to change an individual spirit's path or direction. By doing this, one can change the outcome of another's destiny. One could change the outcome of our whole future.

I had an extraordinary experience when Peter showed me the hall of events, when we stood in front of the Twin Towers after the first plane hit at the World Trade Center. I had started to run with the people there, but then, Peter took me by the arm and told me to stop. I stopped, and I noticed immediately that there was no debris. I felt none of the dust that was all around me. People were frantically running, falling because they could hardly see. But everything was clear to us.

I said, "Peter, I know people in that building!"

When I went to help them, Peter told me, "Bill, you can't help." He looked at me and said, "You're not here yet. This is your future, Bill."

I didn't know what to say, and then, in a blink of an eye, we were transported into my mother-in-law's living room, watching the tower come down. I stood there in the room, watching my wife and my mother-in-law and myself by their side, watching TV. After the first tower came down, somehow, I knew the second plane was coming. I started yelling, trying to tell them right before the second plane hit, but I was jolted away in time. Then we stopped. I was sure we were in the Middle East. I believe it was in Baghdad in Iraq, while it was being bombed. Again, I started to run. I guess it was instinct. Peter said, "Bill, stop. Remember you're not here."

This was so real. I remember it like it was yesterday. It felt like I was in a computer screen that was flickering so fast from one event to another event. Peter and I was part of every event.

Back to my thoughts. It is wrong to alter the path of anyone's spirit. The spirit's destiny might have been an important one. All spirits have their own things to learn and lessons to take on in their life's journey.

Some spirits choose to take the wrong path. Since you choose your own path, you may ask yourself, why would someone choose to be evil or a killer of the innocent? These are folks that stray far away from the spiritual path. Once you are in your body, you still have the freedom of choice. It's easy to be seduced by the dark side. These negative forces can influence anyone in most cases. Our guides work to keep us on the right path, but the dark side can be very strong sometimes, and money can be a catalyst to taking the wrong path.

The spirits belief that taking the wrong path can benefit them financially. They may be seduced all the way into taking someone's life for this reason. Some people are just drawn to the dark side because it feels easy. Remember that this side can only produce negative energy. No matter how good something looks or feels, always follow your intuition. It is never wrong and will lead you back to the light and a positive place.

You do have the right to protect yourself however, if you must. Exercise that right. No one has the right to change your path either. Hopefully, if this ever happens, you'll be able to stop the person without taking their life. Some people believe in revenge and follow the old adage "An eye for an eye, tooth for a tooth," and may resort to taking the life of another. What these people do not understand and realize is that this accomplishes nothing. All they've done is taking away the killer's misery and send them back to another life cycle. A possible and just alternative would be to lock the offender up for life with no possible access to anything. Every spirit has a journey to take, and we as human beings don't have the right to take that journey away. Whatever the journey is, a spirit is on their path, and that might be the right one for them.

Look at how the killing of President John F. Kennedy affected our destiny today. We ended up staying in Vietnam ten years longer than we had to. We should've never been there in the first place. One president's life was taken prematurely, and that, in turn, ended up costing thousands of additional lives.

Martin Luther King Jr. was a great man that wanted peace and equality for all mankind. He, too, was assassinated. We have no way of knowing what he would have accomplished or how our world may have changed if he was alive.

I understood at a higher level than I ever had before. There were very grave concerns from our spiritual guardians.

Peter said to me, "Do you remember when you were eighteen years old and you were jumped by six older men, and one of them had a long knife across your throat. Remember how his friends were yelling, 'Cut him! Cut him!' and you yelled out, 'God, help me'?"

"How could I forget? I thought I was going to get killed!" I responded.

I remembered that the guy with the knife suddenly just dropped his hand, took the knife off my throat, pushed me, and told me to stay out of their neighborhood. I looked at Peter, "That was you, wasn't it?"

"Yes, it was me," Peter responded. "When you asked God for help, your guardians came."

The Lord will keep you from all harm he will watch over your life.

—Psalm 121:7 (NIV)

Peter also said that the concern among all the guardians was at a level that it has not been since the great wars of the past. There is so much negative energy in the world today with all the hate and fear, instead of trust and love.

The concern that Peter references is the concern that our country's freedoms and beliefs were about to be taken from us. A manipulation that started many years ago—our whole society being indoctrinated through subliminal messaging through media, the educational system, and so much more. Through fear and control, they have created a society of sheep being led to the slaughterhouse.

In the last seventy years of history, we've watched these kinds of plans fail over and over. Think about the situations in Cuba, Russia, Venezuela. This threat is quite literally the Antichrist: communism.

Now, imagine a world so barbaric that people feed off of each other's weaknesses. A world of hopelessness and despair. A world of poverty and hate.

I said to Peter, when we were talking about it, "It sounds like the movie *Mad Max* or the book *Nineteen Eighty-Four*," but we're living in it.

Peter said that we, as humans, are at the crossroads now. This crossroads is the choice between love and evil. This applies to everyone, all religions, all faiths—what's the answer?

Remember what I said earlier—don't let them divide us. These are choices we have to follow for our true path of light and love.

CHAPTER 19

The Second Principle of Enlightenment— Your Warnings and Intuitions

The more you faithfully listen to the voice within you,
the better you will hear what is sounding outside.
And only he who listens can't speak.

—Dag Hammarskjold

The warnings and intuitions. The warnings are signals from our spiritual guides and our guardians. We are always being watched. Peter explained to me that we are never alone, that we are looked after from the moment we arrive until the moment we depart for home. Everything is planned out for us. We are warned what direction we should take. Warnings are signs that manifest as intuition.

I remember Peter and Oron repeating to me so many things. My thirst for this knowledge was so overwhelming to me that the more information I received, my thirst seemed to continue to increase. It was unquenchable. I wanted to learn more.

Oron said to me, "A whisper in your ear is an invitation to move toward the path of light. Never let anger steer you in a negative direction." Oron also said that nothing good can ever come from anger, fear, or hate. Actually, these feelings cannot even exist when love is present.

The magnitude of my exhilaration from learning all of these internal truths was illuminating to me.

Listen to the warnings, and they will guide you.

I vividly remember, even though it was a very long time ago, in North Miami Beach State Park, my son Joey was about five years old. Joey was on the edge of a canal, throwing bread into the water to some hungry ducks, as I stood behind him and watched. I am very comfortable around water. I love to swim, snorkel, and scuba dive, but suddenly and out of nowhere, something told me to pull Joey back to where I was standing. This feeling made absolutely no sense to me. The water wasn't deep. So there was no reason for me to feel that Joey might have been in any danger. But my intuition, my guides, Peter and Oron, were suddenly pulling Joey away from the water by guiding my hands. Thank God I listened. Less than a minute later, a nine-foot alligator lunged out of the water. It happened so fast that I didn't see it coming. The alligator grabbed one of the ducks in his mouth, slid back, and looked at us as he disappeared back into the water. If I didn't listen to my intuition that day, it might've been my son Joey taken by that alligator.

The web we weave in our lives takes us in many different directions. One of the most important things that happened to me after my NDE was that my intuition became so acute. My senses felt like they were multiplied many times, and my number sequence that manifests as an alert system in my life made sense.

For example, the way I felt when my wife and I arrived in Bangkok, Thailand, in 1988. We left the airport in a taxi, and I had a very bad feeling. I didn't understand where it came from because we just left China and Hong Kong and were in Korea the week before. Everything was going well with the vacation and the business with the manufacturers. I didn't understand these deep intuitions at that time. But we almost lost our lives that day. I let those feelings pass, as Bangkok was our last leg of the trip.

We had gone there to meet with some of our sterling silver jewelry manufacturers. When we landed at the airport, a government tourism department greeted us, and we decided to set up some tours. We wanted to go to the Grand Palace, see the Buddhist temples, take part in the 007 boat ride, and go to the floating market. We passed through customs, and I declared a substantial amount of money and samples of jewelry that I had in my possession that we had bought in China, Hong Kong, and Korea. The first day in Bangkok went fine, and I forgot about the feeling I had after I left the airport.

The next day, we embarked upon our tours. A guide was accompanying us, and we had her and her driver for the whole day. The guide was a very young lady named Millie that had just graduated college and then worked for the government tourism department. Millie picked us up right in front of our hotel with her driver. First, we went on the 007 boat ride into the floating market of beautiful flowers. She was amazing. She explained all the history of Bangkok and Thailand. I told Millie that we felt so lucky to get her as our guide. I would discover how lucky we were later that day. Millie also told us how she grew up and about her schooling. We told her about the US, and our business part of the trip in Bangkok, how we were buying the sterling silver yesterday.

It was early afternoon, and we had just reached a Grand Palace. We had to remove our shoes and placed them in bins outside before we entered. The tour with Millie was absolutely incredible. After it was over, I went to find my Reeboks in the bin outside and discovered they were missing. A Thai guard from the palace came running up to us and said in a very broken English, "Your Reeboks, your Reeboks."

He had us follow him into the guardhouse in the palace. When we entered the room, my sneakers were on the floor. A man was kneeling on his knees, bowing up and down, and speaking in Thai. I asked Millie what he was saying, and Millie said he was talking about how sorry he was and how he was asking for forgiveness. The guards were acting like this was a big, serious crime. I told Millie to tell the guard to let the man go, and I'll just put my shoes on and leave. The guards turned around and told Millie that he committed a crime in the Grand Palace and that it was punishable by imprisonment. I told Milly to again tell them that we would like to leave and to please let the thief go, as I did not want to press any charges. The guards said, "He cannot leave, and the American cannot leave."

Millie explained to us that we would be required to file a report at the tourism police station and that they told her that the thief must be punished. At this time, they urged my guide Millie to take my wife, Bernadette, back to our hotel, that they would drive me there when they were finished with me at the police station. Luckily for me, my wife and Millie refused. About an hour later, an unmarked car pulled up, and out stepped a Thai soldier and an Australian man that reminded me of James Bond. *Finally, someone that speaks English.* I asked the Australian man what was going on, that I demanded to know. "We're visiting your country, and now we're being detained," I said angrily.

The Australian man told me that he was taking me to the tourism police station to sign some papers. They tried once again to separate me from my wife and Millie by urging her to drive my wife back to the hotel. They both again refused to leave me behind, so we all got into the car, and they drove through Bangkok until we reached the outskirts of the city. I saw signs that said *Leaving Bangkok.*

I asked why we were leaving Bangkok, and the Australian man didn't even turn toward me to reply back. A half hour more of driving went by, and we turned off the road onto some side road back into the hills. Instead of a police station, it was a house in the jungle. That feeling I had when we first arrived in Bangkok was back but worse. There were guards with machine guns in the doorways, and the house had no furniture.

There was only one desk in the room, with three chairs at it and a light hanging from the ceiling. I heard someone being dragged across the floor near our room. I turned around, and I saw the guards dragging the thief through the hall. He was carted off to another room. The guards started questioning me.

"Why are you here in Bangkok?" the colonel asked. He was sitting at the desk with a little cigarette, dangling out of his mouth. The whole thing looked pretty bad. Bernadette and I were sitting across from him, and Millie was standing behind us.

Millie was speaking to him in Thai, and she told us this was their procedure, but I knew something was definitely wrong. I started to get up to leave, and one of the guards came running over and hit me on my back and shoulders with his machine gun. Bernadette started crying. The colonel started asking me about how much money and jewelry I had. At this point, I thought we were going to be killed. The only way they could've known this was from the declaration I did at the airport, and I didn't know if Millie was involved or not. Either it was some kind of scam, or we were in a dangerous position.

One more time, they asked Millie to leave with Bernie. They told her that our driver was waiting outside. Again, they stood fast and told them that they were not leaving me behind. I didn't know what to do at this point. There was no way we could get away if we started to run. Millie started yelling at them in Thai. I don't know what she said. A man came in the room with a stack of papers and said, "You sign."

I asked to call the US Embassy. The last thing I wanted to do was endorse papers in a language I couldn't read or understand, but we were desperate.

Millie looked into my eyes, and she said, "Bill, trust me. I will read every page and translate it into English."

I looked back at her, and something told me to trust her. She read the papers one by one, and I signed some. She said that, so far, they were all about the man stealing my sneakers in the Grand Palace. Then she stopped. She must have read something that she didn't understand or that didn't look right. She told me not to sign them.

I could see in her face that she knew something was wrong now. She started arguing with the colonel.

She turned and whispered, "Bill, I want you and Bernie to get up and start heading for the front door. I will be right behind you. Don't run but walk quickly."

So we both got up, and Millie jumped quickly between me and the Thai soldiers. They were all yelling at each other. This little Thai girl had so much nerve and guts. I couldn't believe it.

As soon as we stepped out the front door, Millie said, "Run."

The driver was about seventy-five feet away, and we ran off to the car. We all got in, locked the doors, and sped away.

I was worried all the way back to Bangkok and back to the hotel. Millie kept on apologizing to us for what happened. I came to the conclusion that the reason why they wanted to separate us was to shake me down for the money I had and probably for my gold presidential watch, and Millie agreed with me.

Thank God Millie and Bernadette refused to leave me that day. They probably would've found me in a ditch somewhere. It was night when we arrived back at the hotel, and we still had the feeling that they might come back for us at any time. I immediately got on the phone to try to book the next flight out of Bangkok. I didn't care where it was flying to. I just wanted to get on a plane and get out of there. It took a while, and it cost me $3,500, but we were able to catch a flight at 5:00 a.m. to Japan, then on to the United States. We knew that we had to leave, and this time, I was wise enough to heed the warning. It took three days for Bernadette and me to stop shaking.

Intuition is not to be ignored, and the results can be dramatic if you do. Intuition is a gift from our guardians. They will guide you in the direction you need to take.

About a year after the Bangkok trip, we were in Los Angeles doing a gift show. I was staying at the Bonaventure Hotel in Downtown Los Angeles. The Bonaventure's garage was underground, and my car was on the third level down. I was riding the escalator down to my car, and all of a sudden, I heard footsteps running fast down the escalator stairs and stopped immediately behind me. I felt that danger was very close even before he stopped. I turned and jumped up one step. His hand was holding a weapon in his pocket, but I was much bigger and had leverage over him, so I grabbed his hand with the gun and bent him over the escalator rail. We were face-to-face.

His eyes were dark and sinister. I yelled right in his face, "Don't even think about it."

I had him pinned and had full control over his hand with the gun in it, and I had my other hand on his throat. Right then, a couple came through the garage doors. I pushed him off the escalator. He hit the floor and looked up at the people, who had started running out of the garage.

Intuition and warnings pave a trail that you should follow. When you veer off the path, it could be dark and scary. The territory is unmarked, and it's easy to become lost. Listen to your inner voices, and you need never fear.

Our heart and soul have their own music and rhythm. The echoes from our guardians should never be dismissed with the wave of a hand. They reverberate throughout all eternity. They are the sounds of God.

If you listen to your heart and soul, they will never lead you astray. Intuition is the touchstone of our guardians. Learn to hear their whispers, and you will follow them. When you tune yourself to the sounds, you will live as lightly and as freely as the wind blows through the leaves of a tree. Your heart will soar, and you shall receive whatever it is that you dream of.

CHAPTER 20

The Third Principle of Enlightenment— Choices

Commit your work to the Lord,
Your plans will be established.

—Proverbs 16:3 (ESV)

The power of choice. I was cautioned that our nation stands at a crossroads. Reality could mean self-destruction. There are very grave concerns from our spiritual guardians that our Lord Jesus is extremely concerned about.

Remember these crossroads. It's our choice—love or evil. Love is everything. It's family—the light of God—watching our children grow, putting a smile on someone's face. Love is helping someone in distress—the light that flows into your heart when you have completed a service for humanity. Love is a flower blooming in the sunlight; it's protecting Mother Earth.

Evil is only hate, fear, and division. When you put politics aside, people would choose love at an astounding rate. Most of everyone would agree that we want a safe world for our children to grow up in. The natural human inclination is love, no matter the political party, no matter the faith or religion, no matter the upbringing.

Oron explained in these words: "Love, not hate. We shall give, not take. Service to one another heals. For service and giving will enlighten our world once again. Our spirits grow through a learning process of choice. We gain knowledge by our mistakes that we correct. And our spirit grows and prospers."

I asked him if the choice was always our own.

Oron said, "God gives us this power. When the spirit chooses the right path, it has completed a lesson."

We are given wisdom so that we can determine right from wrong. Oron said to me that we are all paintings of our own soul. We are voices from the past, present, and future. Our life is a statement about the choices we have made—be they positive or negative. He added that our state of life and our happiness stand in direct proportion to the type of thoughts we've chosen to engage in and in our belief system.

Whatever happens in our lives, good or bad, is a direct result of the choices we have made and the thought processes we have chosen to entertain. There are no accidents in our life. We are not victims of circumstance. If we are victims, it's only because we've chosen to be. We choose our own life. We choose our destiny. We can choose to be noble. We can choose to rise above.

Oron told me, "We can choose the only choice there is, and that is to be one with the universe, to be one with ourselves, to be one with God and all mankind. If you do harm to another, the harm comes back to you. In reality, you only harmed yourself. It does no good to hate or fear. It does no good to seek revenge, as there is no revenge except upon one's self."

Life is a canvas with lessons to be learned. Be alert for those lessons and have your paintbrush ready. Open your mind and open your heart. When you do, you shall see the colors appear before your eyes with a magnificent stroke of inspiration. Now I remember the importance of those comments that the guardians made to me, like the one that states that God gives our spirit power when it chooses the right path.

I graduated with an art degree. I love to draw and paint. It's a blessing that was given to me from God that I have neglected. Something was missing in my heart for quite some time. I worked for so long in my jewelry business, not following my own path, which was art. I neglected that path, and it left an emptiness within my heart—a void that had to be filled. I felt immediately whole again when I took a year off to get back to my oil painting. I believe that through my inspiration for art and painting, I could express things to the world in magnificent colors.

Oron said that our spirits grow when we are on the right path. There is a great force in the universe, one of both positive and negative energy. For a spirit to grow, we have to stay on the positive plain. The negative one might seem very appealing or an easy way out, but it will never help our spirits grow. It only sets us back.

Remember that it's always possible to change directions. If you steer off your path, sometimes it's hard to tell the difference between the right and the wrong. We must rely on our instincts and our intuitions.

Listen to your intuition. It's a message from our guardians, leading us down the right path.

CHAPTER 21

The Fourth Principle of Enlightenment— Service

It's not how much we give but how much love we put in to giving.

—Mother Teresa

To give of yourself is the greatest gift. Every encounter happens for a reason. That reason may be good or bad, right or wrong, positive or negative. The most important thing is for your spirit to learn a valuable lesson and begin to ascend to a higher level of growth, achievement, and wisdom.

The greatest achievement for us as a society is giving in a form of service. Giving of yourself is an action that begets love at the highest level. It will bring you right into the arms of God.

Service is a gift you give back to humanity. When we give, we will receive. Though one should not give just to receive something in return. One gives, shares, helps in order to become a better human being. Without this, life would be shallow and meaningless. Without the giving of ourselves, we would stagnate and become superficial.

Oron told me that if we never gave of ourselves, we would be denying the lessons of our life. We would be denying our chosen path to our souls. He said that the gift of service means to help and to give without asking or expecting anything in return. Our spirits will grow when we give ourselves without question. He also said that service can be simple things like helping an elderly person put their bags from the grocery store in their car.

The things that are most important are helping someone in distress. I was brought back to my paramedic days when my family and I were at one of the Disney water parks and someone went into a seizure. I immediately jumped into action. I held him in my arms and secured his head so he would not crack it on the ground. I placed a little wedge of clothing on the side of his mouth between his teeth so he would not bite his tongue off and to make sure his airway was clear. I held him there until he came out of his seizure. After I did that, his family came up to me and thanked me. I was happy to help though; I was never looking for compensation or something in return.

Your service is important, so please don't be afraid to stop and help if you see someone in distress. One person had asked me if I was afraid. I said no because I was trained, but even if I wasn't, I would have at least tried.

There are higher levels of service as well. They begin when you go out of your way to give of yourself. Volunteer work is a good example of this. Maybe they need some extra help at the hospital, church, school. Maybe you can help feed the hungry and the poor. This will create a positive level of enlightenment in your life, and in turn, it helps produce a force of positive energy in your soul.

There are people who make a life from their gift of service and giving. These people are angels and saints in God's eyes.

Look at Mahatma Gandhi. By his own account, he was born a simple man, shy and fearful. He was transformed by his personal relationship with God. Gandhi believes that nonviolence is the greatest force at the disposal of mankind. It is mightier than the mightiest weapon of destruction devised by mankind. He grew to earn the title *Mahatma*, which means "great soul."

Think of Mother Teresa. In 1948, she found a woman, who was half dead, lying in front of a hospital in Kolkata. She stayed with the woman and comforted her until she died. From that moment on, she dedicated most of her life to helping the poorest people in India and went on to win the Nobel Peace Prize.

Consider a woman named Maria Esperanza. She founded the Betania shrine in Venezuela where many miracles of healing take place. It is believed that the Blessed Mother spoke to Maria in visions. Maria was actually able to cure two-year-old boy Ryan Holick of spina bifida.

When you reach this level of giving and service, your whole life becomes devotion. These people are the modern-day saints, and these miracles are sent to us by our Lord and savior Jesus Christ. Service to others is one of the highest levels of enlightenment to human beings. This giving of yourself will lead you down the path of the master level of enlightenment.

We don't always plan this path; sometimes, it just happens. Consider my near-death experience: one day, I was a businessman at a trade show in Tucson, Arizona—the next, I was tasked with sharing my experience with the world, telling everyone about these nine principles. Suddenly, I was aware of the divine enlightenment of God, and my life was changed.

There is always a reason for everything, although we might not be able to see the reason at that time. Some of the most important services that one can do for humanity just happens that way.

CHAPTER 22

The Fifth Principle of Enlightenment— Ask God to Enlarge Your Wealth, and He Will Enlarge Your Spirit

Oh, that you would bless me in deed and in large my territory.
That your hand would be with me; and that
you would keep me from evil.
That I may not cause pain.

—Chronicles 4:9–10

The basic core of all world religions is love. We are all God's children. I believe in Christianity and our Lord Jesus Christ. But who am I to say that one religion is right and another is wrong? Again, we are all children of God, and God is love, and we are one. Remember what Jesus said: "Even if you don't believe in me, believe in the things I say and do."

A while back, I started looking into the core beliefs of different religions. Almost all religions have the same concept: the idea that there is only one God, and the principal premise is love. Love is the true religion. God is in all of us. So when you have the basic foundation of love, then you're on the right path.

Jesus shared his love with humanity. I believe the basic values inherent in all religions are in accord and genuine.

> *Christianity*
> God is love, and he who abides in love abides in God, and God is with him and in him.
> *Buddhism*
> Hate is never diminished by hatred; it is only diminished by love.
> *Judaism*
> The most beautiful thing a man can do is to forgive wrongness. Thou shall love thy neighbor as thyself.
> *Hinduism*
> Treat others as you would like to be treated. Seek the wisdom by doing service. Service is the highest form of love.

Are all these religions really so different? When we realize that we are not separate entities and we are all part of an unbroken circle of energy, we will truly grow to enlightenment by being one with God. We grow and prosper.

There is only one race—it's called the human race.

CHAPTER 23

The Sixth Principle of Enlightenment— Seek the Lessons

I f you wish to become a great spirit in this life, you must take on as many lessons as you can. Every morning, ask yourself what lessons will be sent to you today. Ask God in prayer.

Oron said lessons are sent to help expose us to new territories and open our boundaries. One must take new and different chances whenever possible. You must learn to move beyond your comfort zone. If you feed on your ideas, they will become your reality. God gives you many chances in the form of lessons each and every day. All you must do is look for these chances and apply them. Any idea can be a good idea, but ideas involve implementation. You must work on them. Don't just let your idea fade away. The best way for you to achieve this is to write it down, all of them, and then begin to work on them. Stick to the ones that really move you. We expand our boundaries and territories in this life by experiencing these chances to act, to learn a lesson. I'm working on this as I write this book.

After my reunion with my guardian angels, who watch over me, protect me, and guide me, I started listening to my inner voices, and I started paying close attention to my new thoughts and ideas. I've found that nighttime is when I'm most in touch with the other side. One night, about a year after my NDE, I was still in the jewelry and watch business, and an idea came to me. I wanted to put angels on watches, and at that time, this hadn't been done before. The first thing I did when I woke in the morning was to write the idea down. The next thing I did was to actually visualize my watch. I started drawing pictures of the Raphael angels on a pendant watch—the case made of leucite, surrounded by gold with floating stars, and half-moon crystals floating around the watch that set off to the right. I brought my pictures to my jewelry manufacturers, and within three weeks, I had my samples made up and manufactured. Ready for sale. Only one month after that, I received an order from QVC for 10,000 pieces. This order was one of ten. So the actual sale was for 100,000 pieces of my angel watch pendant. By the way, my first order sold out in less than twenty minutes of its television preview.

This concept works fast if you allow it to. Listen to your inner voices and follow them. Take every idea that comes into your mind as the gift that it was intended to be.

The world will be given to those who seek and desire it and are willing to take the action necessary to achieve it. An idea is an opening. Anything is possible if you listen and are willing to work at it.

CHAPTER 24

The Seventh Principle of Enlightenment— Unleash the Power of Love

The power of love.

When I passed over into the spiritual world, words cannot convey the infinite level of warmth, love, and peace I felt in my soul. Oron told me that this love is like the air that we breathe. It is the illuminating light of our total existence.

When you love fully and fearlessly without reservation or question, you are freely accepted in the spiritual world, along with your guardians. Our guardian angels and our spirit guides are the noble ones. It is the light and the spirit of God that is illuminating within them with wisdom and knowledge. They possess God's greatest gift to us because within them are the answers to all mankind.

You may feel that this kind of love is impossible to achieve, but nothing could be further from the truth. It is simple in form and essence. God has given us all the tools to work with. All we have to do is listen. Listen to his whispers through our guardians of light.

Oron told me, "Begin by thinking about what the word *love* means to you. Is it a feeling you have for another? A child, a mother, a brother or sister, or a lover? Look a little deeper, and you'll discover that love is everything in one's life. Love is part of our inner soul. For you to achieve love, all you have to do is practice love."

"How do I practice love?" I asked.

"Love is found in a gesture. Love manifests itself as a respect for all living things. Love is a reverence for life," Oron explained.

"So, all I have to do is good deeds?" I asked confusedly.

Then Oron asked me, "Why do we do good deeds? When you can answer the why, you have entered into the wisdom of the light. The great guardians of light have been around for thousands of years—all have mastered love and time. These guardian angels have obtained the highest level in heaven. They are the chosen ones."

Look at the meaning of Jesus's teachings. He mastered these words thousands of years ago: we are one, and love is all. To become love, all we have to do is practice love. When humans listen to Jesus Christ, our teacher, they begin to understand the meaning of love and life, that we are all the sons and daughters of God.

Our guardians teach us that service and giving, even at a small level, like smiling to a stranger, can change the world. Giving back can be also a huge undertaking, like finding a cure for cancer, but let's start with a smile. This is a gift that's easy to give. You will find that if you smile a lot, you begin to transfer your love. You feel better in your heart because when you are smiling, it's impossible for negative feelings to exist. If you don't believe me, try it. Smile. Now attempt to feel sad or depressed without taking the smile off your face. It's just not possible to do because the smile is a transfer of love. Smile at the world, and you will feel better each and every day.

Now, at the ladder of love, take the next step. You could combine a gesture with the smile. You could help someone with a chore without asking for anything in return. You could help someone in distress. If someone asks for assistance, be it family, friends, or a stranger, don't hesitate, just help. Love is more than just your thoughts; it's your actions. This may involve a little work, but it will make your spirit grow by leaps and bounds. Once you start practicing this, you will find that you want to do it again and again.

When Antonia first brought me home to the spiritual world, I noticed all the spirits going and coming. Antonia said that they all have their jobs. I could tell that they were so happy doing them. It was service that they were happy doing—helping, giving, trusting one another. She told me that I had other family members here, like Peter and Oron, that when we pray for God's help, he sends our guardians to help us. She then explained to me that she was my great-grandmother on my father's side, and our families travel together. She was my guardian that brought me home and also delivered me into my human body, both at my birth and my return to my body after my near-death experience.

Antonia said to me, "Bill, this is love at its highest level—working in service of our Lord Jesus Christ."

"Antonia, I feel love like I've never felt before," I said to her.

"Bill, you are love," she said happily.

I looked down at myself, and I was a beautiful beam of glowing light. I was love, peace, and happiness.

Back to my story, let's say that you climbed one more step up the love ladder. When you learn to share, sharing helps you grow because, when you share, selfishness cannot exist. Sharing is a gesture of love, and to be selfish in your life will slow your level of ascension down. The more we give, the more we will receive. But remember, the real reason for giving is not just to receive.

Do not worry too much about money. Money is nice to have, but it will not make your spirit grow. It's not wrong to make money, as long as you don't take advantage of someone else to earn that money. The object of money is to improve the quality of your life and other people's lives.

We're nearing the top of the ladder now. We've arrived at true love. This is the level of love that marriage celebrates. Be there for each other's problems, nurture and respect one another, and learn to forgive. Learn to release and forgive. Don't throw stones at one another.

Forgiveness is a type of love in itself. God does not judge this way, and we, in turn, do not have the right to judge another human being. Forgiveness is a stepstone on the road to enlightenment. When two like-minded souls combine their energy and work together in harmony, they create a third level of energy. This energy is powerful and the gateway to the universe.

"Love begets love," Oron told me.

Humanity and nature begin with the correct loving of one human being. True love transforms you. True love can open doors and take you to heights that you never thought possible.

Now, we've climbed to the top of the ladder—what do you see? One of the highest forms of love that we frequently overlook is the love of Mother Earth. We need to honor and protect her. She is a wonderful spirit; she is our home. She lives and breathes and gives us life. We must take her hand and shelter her from the storm. Without her nourishment, we would cease to exist.

Oron said to me once on a nice summer day, "I invite you to take a walk with her."

I promise you, if you do that, you will never look at a plant, a tree, or a flower in the same way again. Stop to admire a flower, breathe in its scent, feel its petals, ask yourself how it was made. It was created from the love that Mother Earth gives. We are fortunate to have this beautiful Earth on which we live and hereby reap the knowledge that is necessary to help our spirits grow. We are blessed to live so that we can learn to love.

CHAPTER 25

The Eighth Principle of Enlightenment— The Body Is a Temple

Or do you not know that your body is a temple of the
Holy Spirit within you, whom you have from God? You
Are not your own, for you were bought with a price,
So glorify God in your body.

—Corinthians 6:19–20 (NIV)

Your body is your temple. God does not want us to damage our body in any way. Oron told me that it is our vessel that we sail from birth until your passage home.

The ideal is to be able to maximize its use for as long as possible. We should treat our bodies well so that we can prolong the time that we're here to learn. Every minute that we spend on earth helps our spirits grow. Destroying our body with drugs, alcohol, cigarettes, or mutilation is not only unhealthy but also in an abomination.

Our bodies are one of God's gifts to us. Keep the body safe so it can take you on your journey. It's your vehicle. Your body can take you to amazing places, as you can choose to steer yourself in many different directions, but you need to keep it in the best condition possible.

When I was younger, I would sometimes abuse my body and put it at risk with alcohol and drugs. When I started to see my friends overdosing and killing themselves, I began to wake up and consider the consequences. I can't count the number of funerals I went to before I was eighteen. Thank God I never tried hard drugs like heroin. I've seen it destroy so many lives. It's a drug that will lead you to only one of four scenarios: jail, the hospital, a mental institution, but it will ultimately lead to death.

Some are overly concerned with their body image. I've seen young, beautiful girls become bulimic or anorexic in pursuit of the ideal body. Unfortunately, this can be very detrimental physically.

Above all, it's a person's inner beauty that is truly important. True beauty radiates from our soul. The body is merely a vessel that we live in. No matter what you look like or what shape you're in, God loves you.

It is most important to keep your body from harm for the sake of our children. We should be there to hug them, squeeze them, and tell them that we love them each and every day. It's so important to their life if they are to become well-adjusted. You are your children's leader, their shepherd. You must lead them down the right path.

When it comes to the body, keep it, use it, love it, and respect it. It will take you on God's journey to all the wonderful places your spirit will seek.

CHAPTER 26

The Ninth Principle
of Enlightenment—
Protect Mother Earth

Mother Earth is your spirit. She gives us life. She is our heart and soul. She is the birth mother of humanity.

This earth does not belong to us; we belong to her. She is the force that connects us all. Her influence extends from the trees and the plants that provide us with oxygen to the vast supply of water that nourishes us and makes all living things grow. She is the jugular vein of our existence. We must protect her, and she, in turn, will protect us and give us life.

When you stop and consider the beauty here, it's amazing—the majesty of her mountains, the bounties of the plains, the turbulent and tempestuous oceans. When we accept Mother Earth as one of the great spirits, we will come to understand what makes us one with the earth.

Stop and marvel at the miracles she creates every day. Take a look at the food on your table—Mother Earth supplied it. The water we drink is her offspring. The air we breathe comes directly from her nostrils. She is the entity we draw our life's breath from.

She takes care of us and the entire animal kingdom. There is a place for everyone and everything here. She's here to help supply us with a beautiful life, so be careful with any abuse done to her, as she is not ours for the taking. When we remove from her body, we must replace. The same applies to the animal kingdom. Do not destroy what you will not use for food. Remember that every animal also has its own path to follow.

Listen to her voice in the wind that speaks of higher places of enlightenment. Watch her rivers flow, and you will know that this is her strength that flows to the sea. Picture yourself as an angel and glide above the mountain peaks and plains, across the vast and beautiful oceans. You will come to feel that you are one with the earth and the earth is one with you.

Love her and respect her, for she holds the voice of reason that we must obey and honor. I remember, back in the spiritual world, Peter told me, "Billy, Mother Earth feels."

"What do you mean by she feels?" I asked.

"She feels everything that's going on in this world—hate, wars, the greed. It's tearing the world apart. When there is too much disturbance in the balance of the earth, it creates a negative imbalance within the earth itself," Peter responded. "Sometimes, the negative energy can get so bad that she creates storms, tornadoes, earthquakes. She responds," he added.

Peter then told me that, at times, the guardians would have to step in to stop destruction. They stepped in during the early atomic bomb and hydrogen bomb years because our world was not ready for this yet and is still not ready. Instead of making weapons of destruction, we should be feeding the poor.

I didn't quite understand everything that he told me that day, but what resonated with me the most was that Mother Earth feels. At that time, my mind was opening up to so much knowledge, and it just made me want to learn more.

Peter said at this point, "That's enough for now."

When I asked if there was more that I didn't know, he said that there was so much more knowledge than I could ever imagine.

What I took from my conversation with Peter was that humanity must slow down and spend time on a positive plane. Otherwise, we could be heading for some scary times.

Later on in my time in the spiritual world, Peter asked me, "Billy, remember the teaching of service and giving?" When I said that I did, he continued, "Well then, you're on the right path, but humanity has to change."

I stood there. I knew that his thought wasn't complete yet.

"Bill, you're here for a reason. You will be a messenger. We have used people before," he said.

"Peter, why me? I'm home now, I can't! I'm home, and I want to stay!" I pleaded.

I knew this was important though—Peter had never called me Bill before.

He said to me, "Our world is at a crossroads. We could be heading for the war that ends all wars. The war that ends life as we know it."

"What can I do?" I asked.

"Send a message so strong that it echoes through the mountains and the seas and the valleys: people have to come back to God. They are too far off their path of enlightenment. It's so bad that families are being torn apart. They just don't speak to each other anymore. These are dangerous times. This level of danger can be catastrophic," he responded.

Evil is playing a big part in it. It's taking a hold of people's minds and hearts. It has already happened in many countries around the world—governments taking away fundamental rights of their people to the point where they no longer have access to food, clean water, or medicine, and they are denied the freedom of faith. This evil cannot happen in America. We must stand together, rise together, become one. People, churches of all faiths, must come together, or we can be destroyed and lose life

We are one race—it's called the human race.

"How do I stop it?" I asked Oron.

"Bill, you're the messenger," he responded. "People will come, but they need a voice on earth to lead them back to the light. The human soul was not meant to bow down to evil. It wants to be free."

Just like Peter said, Mother Earth responds to our energy. Have you noticed that there are so many more natural disasters in today's day and age than even twenty, thirty years ago? Floods, droughts, fires, tornadoes, hurricanes—more people are dying because of disasters like these than ever before.

If we managed to set our souls free of greed, fear, hate, Mother Earth will respond as well in a much different way. She is hurting, and we must do our part to emit the positive energy that she so desperately needs.

CHAPTER 27

Antonia's Lessons

There are positive and negative forces. Everything in our universe is made up of energy; it's the basis of our universe. "It is a life force," Antonia explained to me. "The more positive the life force, the more positive the energy is that lies within."

Too much negative energy can dilute the positive force. This applies to all of life's forces. The earth itself responds to positive and negative energy. When there is a disturbance in our force, it is because there are too many destructive acts being committed by large numbers of people.

Negativity breeds negativity and calamity. Positive acts of kindness and love breed a positive and peaceful planet.

I said to Antonia, "Are you telling me that the earth itself has feelings? Because Peter was also trying to explain that to me."

She responded, "Yes, Bill, earth has built-in receptors that respond to positive and negative energies, so yes, the earth feels."

Newton's third law, also known as the Law of Forces, states that when two bodies interact, they apply forces to one another that are equal in magnitude and opposite in direction. This is a great way to think about what kind of energy you put into the universe and what you get back.

I remember the bombing in Baghdad, Iraq. Soon after, I suffered from repeated dreams of tornadoes hitting our country with massive force. I have realized that my dreams were foreshadowing the beginning of an event, a negative energy pull that exists at this time.

About a week after the bombing, the southern parts our country were hit with over 300 tornadoes raining down in many states. So many lives were lost. When lives were taken from the two planes that hit the Twin Towers, years later, we've had outbreaks of Ebola, SARS, COVID-19, AIDS. These viruses have cost millions of lives. This is a negative outcome in a direct response to a negative action.

Any killing of any kind breeds a negative reaction. War that causes thousands of deaths or viruses that cause millions of deaths are devastating to our planet. Any action, whether positive or negative, results in an equal, opposite reaction from the earth.

Antonia's message was very clear to me. This is what we are seeing today. We can alter the disturbances that exist by engaging in positive actions or humanitarian aid. Good deeds need to commence immediately.

CHAPTER 28

Choices, Messages of Love to Change the Outcome

Darkness cannot drive out the darkness, only light can do that. Hate cannot drive out hate, only love can do that.

—Dr. Martin Luther King

We have important choices to make. As individuals, we shape and change the destiny of our world. Earth could be utopian. We could live in a world that's filled with love. Hopefully, we can reach this level before it's too late. If we manage to do this, our earth will prosper and progress. Our spirits will grow immensely. Many people will reach master levels of enlightenment.

Could you imagine a world that lives, loves, and works together as one force in the universe? Imagine and believe, and it will exist; this world will be a wonderful, powerful place. Feel and share love the way it was meant to be. Give love freely and without reserve or question. Picture a world with no wars, no hate, and no fear of any kind. Children would feel safe and have no need for protection from the horror that exists today. Men and women would be free to expand their territories and boundaries. Judgments of any kind could not exist. People would be accepted for who they are spiritually, not physically or athletically. This world would be one. Our spirits would be liberated and would be able to grow at an accelerated rate. This is not an impossible goal to reach. It is even easy to obtain if you follow the Principle of enlightenment.

This is a level that we, as human beings, are supposed to reach. There are nine principle s of enlightenment, and they are what God wants for us right now. Life seems to be moving quicker and quicker; people feel they can't keep up with it. No one has time to think, process, or ponder the outcomes of their actions.

Now let me show you another possible future outcome for our world. A world that, unfortunately, looks like we are heading toward. Before I talk about it, keep in mind that we have the power to change the course of the future. Currently, our world is not heading in a positive direction. Wars and government terrorism strike fear at the heart of our society. Endless wars are just causing more and more destruction. Our values are being attacked, and this already seems to be present in everything that we see every day—in movies, in what is being taught to our children in schools. It seems there is evil entity that is taking over our society. All we hear about today is one pandemic after another. COVID-19 started never-ending variants of virus that keep on and on, that seems like it will continue It is an entity that will destroy our families, our friends. People are being blinded with lies and corruption that will totally wipe out the life we knew. It will bring us to a world clouded by negativity and despair. Remember, negativity breeds negativity. This will lead us to total destruction. Imagine now a world so barbaric that people feed off each other's weaknesses, despair, and hopelessness. A world filled with fear, poverty, and hate. Picture the movies *Mad Max* and *The Hunger Games*. Now imagine you are living in it—a world where basic staples like food and clean water are hard to come by, a world where you have to fight to stay alive, a world where people take from one another until there's nothing left to take. It is understandable to fear this world.

We are at a crossroads now; we are at a place where destiny has called us. We can change the path of the world with our actions. Be aware of the choices you make, understand, and follow the positive paths.

Live in the light.

CHAPTER 29

The Messenger

Where do I begin? I feel that we are at a place and time where we can move forward in small steps, where we can help and heal by passing love on to one another with our actions: helping, giving, not hesitating to be there for someone in need.

I've been given a blessing—a gift of light and of love. I stood in the light of God with my guardians. I learned the knowledge and the wisdom of the laws of enlightenment. I have decided to become a messenger of light and love and for God to pass on these gifts that were given to me by my guardian angels. I will teach the nine principle s of enlightenment to everyone in need of them.

We can change the direction that our world is heading into. It's dangerous beyond the crossroads. We have people and families that don't even speak to each other anymore because they have separate beliefs. The first thing I would say is that we must start listening to each other again—but listen with our hearts.

We need our country to get back to being a safe place for our children to grow. We cannot do things like defund our police departments. Yes, we have a lot of work to do for our communities that face racial oppression and discrimination, but without law and order, society will become a free-for-all, completely out of control. We are already seeing it in states like California. A bill was recently passed that would allow criminals to be paid $300 per month with taxpayer money for *not* shooting people. Another state action was paying citizens to turn in their guns, but what stopped people from turning in old, unusable firearms and using that money to buy new ones? There is a lot of backward mentality in the world in today's age, and by listening with our hearts, a lot of the problems we are facing today would be solved in the blink of an eye. People must start listening to each other.

We are in a battle of good against the evil that's trying to tear down our society and is bringing us to a place of massive despair. We have to remember one thing: we are in control.

We as Americans have our Constitution and the Bill of Rights. I will spend the rest of my life fighting for God, my faith, and my country.

One small action by an individual can start a chain reaction. Tell someone about this book. Help someone toward a positive path. They will then be empowered to do the same. The word will spread.

By following our instincts and our intuition, we know what is right. We can change the outcome of our destiny. If we follow our true path, we will live in a world of peace and harmony. I do believe that, in the end, the light will overcome the darkness. This is why I had to tell my story. Please tell others.

God gave us this beautiful earth to live on. Let's not destroy it. Instead, let's make choices every day to make it a positive place to live and love. The world will then fulfill our life cycles and go on and on for thousands of years. God meant for us to have a wonderful life. I will say it one more time—

Love is the way to the light.

ABOUT THE AUTHOR

Bill Tortorella was born in Brooklyn, New York, in 1952, to a coal miner's daughter named Olga. She owned and operated a bar and grill across the street from Ebbets field, where the Brooklyn Dodgers played and many of the ballplayers came in for lunch.

Bill, as a very young boy, recalls hearing the names of Leo Durocher (the manager), Sandy Koufax, and Gil Hodges. Bill's father, Joe Tortorella, was the president of Local 804, the International Brotherhood of the Teamsters. He would relate stories to Bill of conventions he attended in Miami Beach and going fishing for giant kingfish with a friend by the name of Jimmy Hoffa.

Bill graduated the school of art and design in Manhattan with awards for his art. He won the international art contests for WNBC radio and television for the Broadway musical play *Jesus Christ Superstar*, an Andrew Lloyd Webber production. His first job was at Triad Studios New York City, as a commercial artist. He moved to Miami Florida in 1973. The move caused a career change, and he became a paramedic for the county. He attended Mount Sinai medical school. Some years later, a twist of fate brought Bill into his own business and sales where he traveled the world and worked for big companies like Wyndham, as a manager, and Marriott, where he has achieved many awards in his field.

Lightning Source UK Ltd.
Milton Keynes UK
UKHW010610260123
415995UK00001B/185